Treecology

OTHER TITLES IN THE YOUNG NATURALISTS SERIES

Awesome Snake Science! 40 Activities for Learning About Snakes

Birdology: 30 Activities and Observations for Exploring the World of Birds

Insectigations: 40 Hands-on Activities to Explore the Insect World

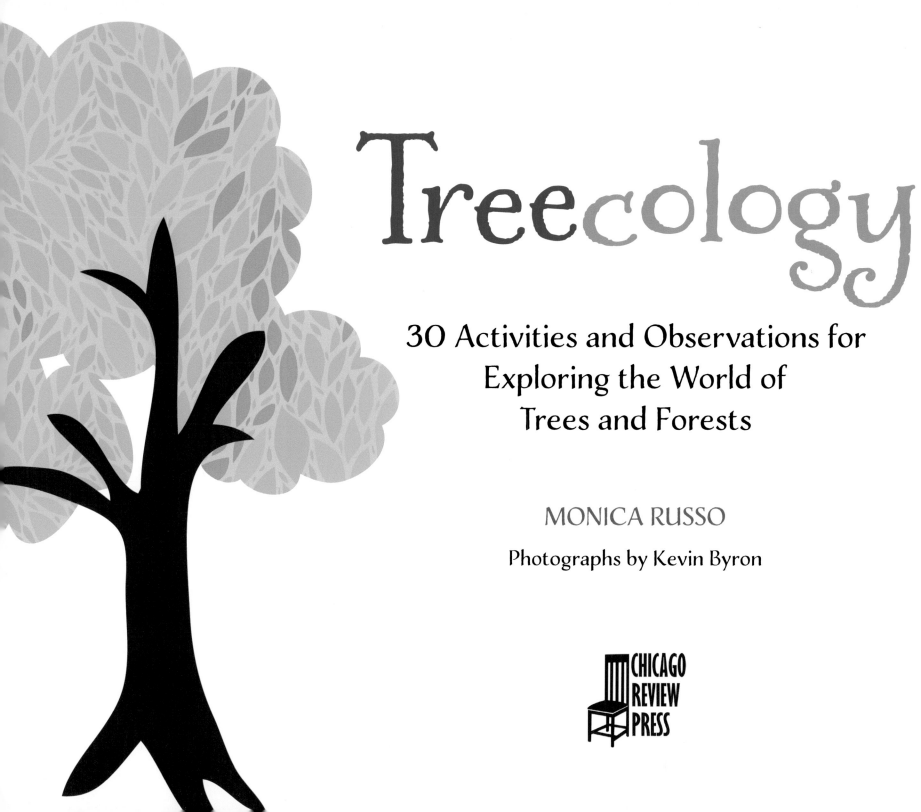

Treecology

30 Activities and Observations for Exploring the World of Trees and Forests

MONICA RUSSO

Photographs by Kevin Byron

CHICAGO
REVIEW
PRESS

Published by Chicago Review Press Incorporated
814 North Franklin Street
Chicago, Illinois 60610

ISBN 978-1-61373-396-7

Library of Congress Cataloging-in-Publication Data
Names: Russo, Monica, author. | Byron, Kevin (Photographer).
Title: Treecology : 30 activities and observations for exploring the world of
    trees and forests / Monica Russo ; photographs by Kevin Byron.
Description: First edition. | Chicago, Illinois : Chicago Review Press
    Incorporated, [2016] | Audience: Ages 7+.- | Includes bibliographical
    references and index.
Identifiers: LCCN 2015050678 (print) | LCCN 2016004779 (ebook) | ISBN
    9781613733967 (trade paper) | ISBN 9781613733974 (pdf) | ISBN
    9781613733998 (epub) | ISBN 9781613733981 (kindle)
Subjects: LCSH: Trees—Juvenile literature. | Trees—Study and teaching
    (Elementary)—Activity programs. | Forest ecology—Study and teaching
    (Elementary)—Activity programs.
Classification: LCC QK475.8 .R8855 2016 (print) | LCC QK475.8 (ebook) | DDC
    582.16078—dc23
LC record available at http://lccn.loc.gov/2015050678

Cover and interior design: Sarah Olson
Cover photos: Kevin Byron
Interior illustrations: Monica Russo
Interior photos: Kevin Byron

Printed in the United States of America
5 4 3 2 1

This book is dedicated to all the ecologists, conservationists, botanists, and educators who work to increase our understanding and appreciation of trees, woodlands, and forest ecology. Without trees, life on Earth as we know it would disappear.

The eastern white pine is the state tree of Maine and Michigan.

Contents

Acknowledgments

This book would not have been possible without Kevin Byron's amazing photographs of trees, forests, and wildlife. They are the result of more than 35 years of fieldwork and technical expertise, and many images have come from once-in-a-lifetime opportunities, sometimes in quite difficult situations. His photos are vital to this book's design and presentation. Kevin has also been our "systems manager," organizing the details of production and communication.

I would like to express my great appreciation of my parents, who were expert at cultivating and maintaining a variety of trees and flowering shrubs, and who encouraged my early interest in nature and science. Many people have helped to create this book. Our friends Dick and Jane gave us unlimited access to their beautiful sanctuary of gardens and woodlands. My sister Sandy told us about the woodland preserves south of us. Several people gave us photo ops of trees, landscapes, wildlife, and special scenes: we thank Eileen, Bob, Brandon, Domenica, Bernie, and Myra.

Our many thanks and appreciation also go to Lisa Reardon, senior editor at Chicago Review Press, for her guidance in the development of this book.

Introduction

Trees can be seen almost everywhere we live: in front of our homes and apartments, around schools and playgrounds, and near libraries. They are planted around shopping malls, parking lots, and office buildings. Even if you have never seen a forest or taken a woodland walk, you might have enjoyed the cool shade of a tree on a hot day or seen the beauty of a tree in flower. Trees also give us visual relief from the city environment. In neighborhood parks and city centers they provide a "greenscape" that offers a pleasant, relaxed experience.

Trees are a vital part of a healthy forest ecology, supporting a diversity of both plant and animal life. They provide homes and food for songbirds and other wildlife—even butterflies! They can create a windbreak, protect watersheds, and help prevent soil erosion.

There are many concerns about forests and trees around the world. Drought, tornadoes, and storms can kill trees or cause severe damage. But human activities cause the most concern to botanists and other scientists. Deforestation and clear-cutting have become very important topics. Large forest areas are cut down to make space for farms, buildings, or roadways. In central Mexico, forest trees have been illegally cut down, probably for lumber or firewood.

Some species of trees have become rare or endangered. In the mountains of Japan, a species of birch tree is nearly extinct in the wild. Fortunately, some of the trees are safe in arboretums. In the tropical habitat of the Amazon in South America, the tree that produces Brazil nuts is becoming rare because of deforestation. And in Europe, coal mining in Germany has destroyed large forested areas, but there is a project to plant new trees.

Trees are symbols of strength and long life. They leave us with pleasant memories and are the inspiration for poetry and art around the world. Trees are natural time machines, revealing the past in fossil evidence and growing with us into the future, through storm and wind and into peaceful bright summer days.

You can observe trees closely throughout the year and appreciate their enormous variety—the difference in the shapes and designs of leaves, the texture of bark, and the many different types of flowers and seeds they produce. You can enjoy the colors of leaves in the fall and the beautiful silhouettes many trees show during the winter. And you can have fun with the activities in this book, as you learn about trees, forests, leaves, and seeds!

Important Note: Never walk in the woods alone. Ask an adult or a few friends to go along. Always tell an adult where you are going, and when. You don't have to visit a large wooded area to do the activities in this book. You can make many discoveries simply by observing trees in your neighborhood, around your school playground, or in a park.

1

What Is a Tree?

Trees are almost everywhere. They are planted along streets and around playgrounds. They create pleasant, cool, shaded areas around homes in the summer. Trees provide food, shelter, and homes for birds and other wildlife. City parks and gardens are valued for their beautiful trees, and forests are enjoyed by hikers, naturalists, campers, and bird-watchers.

Is It a Tree or a Shrub?

Trees—and **shrubs**—are large plants with hard woody trunks or stems. Most have leafy branches or groups of leaves. Size is generally the best way to tell the difference. Shrubs usually grow less than 15 or 20 feet tall and often spread out close to the ground. A mature (fully grown) tree can grow tall and straight to a height well over 20 feet.

Most trees have a single main trunk that branches out into many smaller branches and twigs. But most shrubs have several woody stems rising right from the ground and then dividing into thinner branches. Your school, house, apartment, or nearby grocery store parking lot probably has several shrubs planted around it.

Here are some examples of shrubs:

- flowering lilac
- blueberry bushes
- azaleas
- honeysuckle bushes
- flowering forsythia
- others: hawthorn trees, witch hazels, and sumacs can often grow more than 15 feet tall, so they are described in field guides as small trees or large shrubs. A single plant family can include both trees and shrubs—and even small woodland wildflowers!

It can be confusing to tell a tree from a shrub. Some trees don't grow tall because they are stunted by insect damage or poor growing conditions, such as **drought**. And many trees are pruned and trimmed so that they remain small. Even though they could

(*left*) This large silver maple, planted as a shade tree, is about 40 feet tall.

(*right*) Hawthorns are often described as shrubs or small trees, because they usually grow less than 20 feet tall. This downy hawthorn is in full bloom and about 12 feet tall.

become much taller, they are kept to the size of a shrub (less than 20 feet tall). Here are a few examples:

- Apple trees can grow more than 20 feet tall, but in orchards they are usually pruned and trimmed to keep them smaller to make it easy to harvest ripe apples from them.

- Rhododendrons can grow well over 20 feet high in the wild, but when planted in front of houses or public buildings they are kept trimmed to stay small.

- Hemlock trees growing naturally in the wild can grow 60 to 70 feet tall—with some huge specimens reaching more than 100 feet! But they are sometimes planted in rows near a building and trimmed and pruned to form a low hedge.

- A balsam fir can grow to be a large tree—usually 50 to 60 feet tall. But on a tree farm where Christmas trees are raised and grown, they are trimmed so they can fit inside a house for the holidays. Balsam firs in poor growing conditions may only grow a few feet tall.

On the coast of Newfoundland, Canada, balsam firs are stunted and windblown. Even though they are mature trees, they can't grow very tall. Groups of these stunted, low trees are called **tuckamore**. The tuckamore firs shown here are only about four feet tall.

Rhododendrons are often used for landscaping in front of homes and public buildings. This "rhody" is kept pruned to maintain its shape and size. Several different species (and cultivated varieties) are grown and used for planting.

Parts of a Tree

On the ground at the base of a tree, you can often see the top surface of large roots spreading away from the trunk. If you could dig up a large tree, you would find that the big roots divide into smaller roots, then into tiny rootlets, and finally into tinier roots called root hairs. You can sometimes see the entire root system of a tree when it has been blown down by a severe storm and the roots have been ripped out from the ground.

The trunk of most trees rises upward to spread out into large branches, then smaller branches, and then smaller and shorter twigs. The twigs support buds and leaves.

The leafy top of a mature, fully grown tree is called the crown. The tops of many trees, including maples, birches, oaks, and ash trees, are rounded. An American elm has branches and a crown that grow in a fan or fountain shape. A blue spruce, often planted near homes and buildings, has a

CROWN includes branches, Twigs + leaves

BRANCHES

TRUNK

PARTS OF A TREE

underground roots

American elms are found in most of the eastern and central United States and in parts of southern Canada. This huge specimen is almost 100 feet tall!

The crown of this sugar maple is a beautiful sight in the fall, when the leaves turn bright orange.

triangular shape with a pointy top. Balsam fir trees have a triangular shape too (also called a pyramid shape).

Parts of a Leaf

The flat part of a leaf is called the blade. Some leaves have a very wide blade, like those of the American sycamore, which can be eight inches across. Other leaves are quite narrow. The leaf of a black willow tree is only about one-half inch wide. Pine

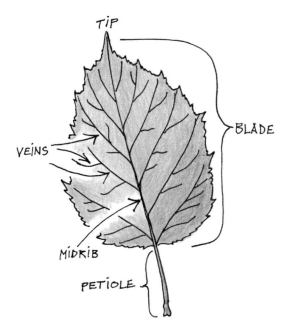

The parts of a leaf. This is the leaf from a white birch, also called a paper birch. White birch is the state tree of New Hampshire and the official tree of the province of Saskatchewan, Canada.

leaves are called needles because they are long and very thin.

Leaves are attached to twigs by a stem called a **petiole** (PET-ee-ole). The petiole on the leaves of elms, chestnuts, birches, and oaks is fairly short. But the petiole on the leaf of a bigtooth aspen or on most maples is long. Look at the petiole on the leaf of any tree or shrub, and observe how long it is. Is the petiole shorter than the length of the leaf blade, or is it longer than the leaf? Bigtooth aspen, cottonwoods, and trembling aspen all have long, flat petioles, which cause the leaves to wiggle in a breeze.

Leaf Shapes and Designs

Leaves have many different shapes. Each **species** (type) of tree has its own leaf shape. There are many different species of maples and birch trees, and the leaves of each species have a distinct shape and size.

Leaves can be long and narrow, like those of willows. They can be oval, like those of cherry and plum trees. Some trees have leaves that come to a long point. The leaves of a white oak have rounded, finger-like lobes. The leaves of sassafras trees can

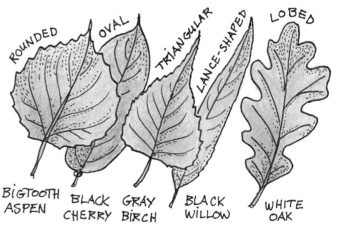

Some different shapes of leaves.

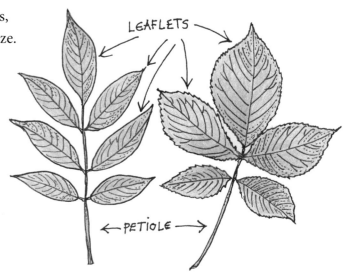

Compound leaves. Each is a single leaf, divided into several leaflets. Each leaflet is attached to the main petiole by a tiny stem. The leaf on the left is from a white ash. The leaf on the right is from a shagbark hickory. Walnut trees and locust trees also have compound leaves.

have three different shapes: a single oval, an oval with a "thumb" (a shape like a mitten), and a three-part leaf. All three shapes can be found on one sassafras tree!

The edge of a leaf also can be important in identification. Some leaves have a mostly smooth edge, like those of a southern magnolia. Others, like red maples and American chestnuts, have a toothed or **serrated** edge.

You may also notice that on some trees (and other plants) the leaves grow from the twigs opposite from each other. On other trees, the leaves are alternating (or staggered) along the branch. Once you start to look at the shape, design, and placement of different leaves, you will develop an eye for noticing details. This will help you to

THE UNDERSIDE OF A LEAF

You need good light indoors for this activity, or a bright day outside.

MATERIALS
- A few different leaves, picked from trees or shrubs
- Magnifying glass

1. Pick a few leaves from different trees or shrubs. (It doesn't matter if you can't identify them.)

2. Compare the upper side of the leaf with the underside. The underside is probably lighter in color.

3. Now look at the underside more closely with a magnifying glass. You will find that the veins are easier to see.

4. Look for a different texture than on the upper side. The underside may be smoother, or it may be rough, fuzzy, or hairy.

(*left*) A few different types of magnifying glasses. The folding one can easily be kept in a pocket and carried on a nature walk. The small twig is from a black spruce.

(*center*) A close-up view of the underside of eastern hemlock needles, showing silvery bands. You can easily see them with a magnifying glass.

(*right*) A close-up view of the fuzz on the underside of a black cherry leaf, along the central vein.

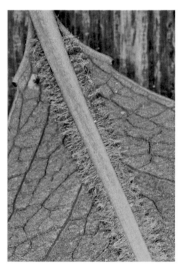

Poison sumac is a shrub or small tree. Never touch a leaf of this plant! This is a very toxic plant, and even a slight touch will cause a skin rash that may need medical attention.

The compound leaf of a poison sumac shrub. Note the reddish central vein and other veins on each leaflet. This photo was taken in October, when the leaves turn yellow and can look quite pretty—but don't touch it!

identify common trees, and to keep a lookout for anything different or unusual.

On the underside of hemlock leaves (which are short, flat "needles"), you can see white or silvery lines on each side of the central vein. These white lines are made up of special cells that surround tiny pores. You can also find white lines on the underside of balsam fir ("Christmas tree") needles.

The underside of a black oak leaf has tiny fuzzy hairs where a vein meets the central vein. It's a good way to tell a black oak from a red or scarlet oak. And the leaves of black cherry trees have rust-colored fuzz at the base of the leaf, just past the petiole.

Collecting Leaves to Make Rubbings, to Press, and to Preserve

When you see an interesting tree, you might want to pick a leaf and preserve it. A fresh leaf can be preserved by pressing and drying it (which can take several days). Or you can quickly make a colorful crayon rubbing of a leaf—to decorate notepaper! This will make a copy of the leaf, so you will always be able to look at its shape and design.

Once you have collected several leaves that you like, you can easily press and dry them so they are preserved. Pressed leaves are often kept in scientific collections in museums and universities. Many are important historic specimens. They

Pressed specimens from a botany collection. Some specimens in museums, universities, and science centers are more than 100 years old!

You need **oxygen** to breathe. So do all other animals. Oxygen is a part of the air all around you, and a lot of it comes from plants—including trees! Plants need some oxygen too, but they depend on **carbon dioxide** (which animals exhale). So, while you breathe in oxygen and exhale carbon dioxide, plants use carbon dioxide and produce lots of oxygen!

MAKE A CRAYON RUBBING OF AN INTERESTING LEAF

Try making crayon rubbings of different leaves in different colors. You can use your leaf rubbings as notepaper or to send a colorful message to a friend.

MATERIALS

- A fresh leaf (any kind)
- Piece of thin cardboard (cardboard cut from a cereal box works best)
- White or light-colored paper
- Bright-colored crayons (like red, blue, or purple)

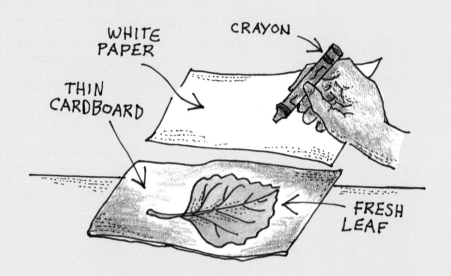

A crayon rubbing of a red maple leaf. Next to it is the leaf of a gray birch—notice the triangular shape and long pointed tip.

1. Place your leaf underside up on top of the cardboard. The underside usually has the strongest veins, which will show up best in a rubbing.

2. Put the white paper over it, and hold down the paper with one hand.

3. Rub the crayon over the petiole first, because it's easy to feel. Then rub all around the edge of the leaf. You'll feel (and see) the edge of the leaf as you color.

4. Go over the entire leaf with the crayon, pressing hard enough so that the shape of the leaf and the veins show up.

5. You might have to try a few different leaves—or crayon colors—before you are satisfied.

6. Use your rubbing as notepaper, a card, artwork, or letter paper.

PRESS LEAVES TO PRESERVE THEM

If you have found some leaves that have a shape you like, it's easy to press them and dry them so you can keep them preserved.

MATERIALS

- Several sheets of newspaper
- Scissors
- 2 or 3 pieces stiff cardboard
- A few freshly picked leaves from trees (or shrubs)
- Something heavy, such as a few heavy books or a flat rock

1. Cut the newspaper pages into several smaller-size squares—about the size of a sheet of printer paper.

2. Place one piece of cardboard on a flat space, like your desk.

3. Lay two or three pieces of newspaper on the cardboard, and place a few of your leaves on it.

4. Cover the leaves with more newspaper. You might need several layers of newspaper to cover more leaves.

5. Put a final piece of newspaper over your last specimens, and add a piece of cardboard to the top. Put something heavy on top of it all—a few books or a rock.

6. Let the leaves dry and press for four or five days, and then turn them over. Let them dry and press again for a few more days.

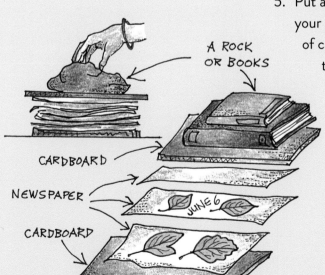

A ROCK OR BOOKS

CARDBOARD

NEWSPAPER

CARDBOARD

JUNE 6

are lasting evidence that certain species were found growing in a particular place. Many specimens in scientific collections were pressed in the 1800s.

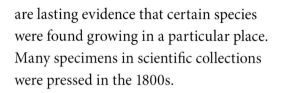

How Many Leaves Are There on One Tree?

The total number of leaves on one tree is different from one species of tree to another, and from tree to tree. But a healthy, large, mature maple or oak tree can have about 200,000 leaves! In contrast to that, a small black cherry sapling, standing about four feet tall, has 172 leaves on it.

MAKE A LEAF SPECIMEN CARD

You can use one of your pressed leaves to make a specimen card that will last for many years.

MATERIALS

- Cardboard
- Scissors
- Plastic sandwich bag
- White paper
- Pressed dried leaf
- Tape
- Marker
- Colored pencils, pens, or crayons

1. Cut the cardboard to fit inside the sandwich bag. Cut it small enough so that the sealing-strip at the end of the bag can be folded over and taped.

2. Cut the white paper to the same size as the cardboard.

3. Carefully place your leaf in the center of the white paper. Stick a small piece of tape across the petiole to hold it in place.

4. Use a marker, pencil, or crayon to write your name, the date, and the place you found the leaf on the paper. Be careful to not touch the leaf—it might crack or crumble!

5. Carefully slide the white paper and leaf into the bag.

6. Slide the cardboard in the bag, under the leaf and white paper.

7. Gently smooth air out of the bag and press the seal at the end closed. Fold the sealed end around to the back and tape it.

   Try making cards using different leaves. You can also draw a colorful border or margin on the white paper, around the leaf, or write a note on it, to give to a friend.

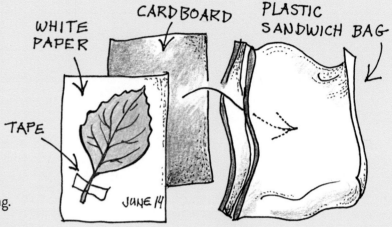

Making a specimen card.

A specimen card made with a pressed leaf from a bigtooth aspen.

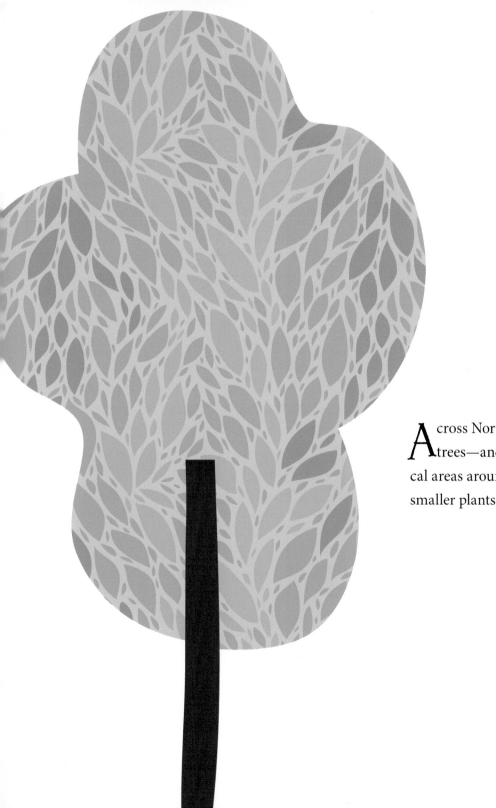

2

‚‚‚‚‚‚‚‚‚‚‚‚‚‚‚‚‚‚‚‚‚‚‚‚‚‚

Tree Families

Across North America, there are more than 70 plant families that include trees—and more are found in Australia, Africa, Europe, China, and tropical areas around the world. While some of those families just include trees, smaller plants are also included—even wildflowers!

Families of Trees

Here are some of the most common tree family groups. It helps to remember that these are plant families, and the members of a family may include trees, wildflowers, shrubs, and even vines.

- **Yew family.** Yews have short evergreen needles, and a bright red berrylike cup surrounding each seed. Only two species of yews are found wild in North America. Species **native** (growing wild naturally) to other countries are grown for landscaping.

- **Pine family.** This includes the many species of pine, spruce, hemlock, and fir. These trees are usually called evergreens, because they look green throughout the year. But they do lose some of their needles every fall, and those get replaced in the spring with new growth.

The long, thin leaves of pine trees are called needles. The needles grow from the twigs in clusters called **fascicles** (FAS-i-kils). The needles on a pitch pine grow in fascicles of three. You can remember that the needles of an eastern white pine grow in fascicles of five by remembering that the word *white* has five letters, *w-h-i-t-e*!

Other species of pines have needles in fascicles of three and five also. Some species have short needles, while others have long needles. Sometimes it's hard to keep track of all the different types of pines! But it's fun to get a start in observing the details of pine trees.

Botanists (scientists who study plants) call trees in the pine family **conifers**, because they produce woody, scaled cones with seeds inside. Conifers have cones of different sizes: white pines have cones about six to eight inches long, but the eastern hemlock has much smaller cones—less than an inch long.

- **Redwood family.** The famous coast redwood of California and Oregon is a member of this family, along with the giant sequoia. Another member is the metasequoia, also called the dawn redwood. It is a native, wild tree in China but has been grown in nurseries and is sometimes planted around homes.

The cones of an eastern hemlock.

- **Bald cypress family.** This family includes many of the trees found in the swamps and marshes of Florida and the extreme southeastern United States.
- **Cedar family.** One member of this family, the northern white cedar, is also called arborvitae (ar-bor-VY-tee). It is native to the northeastern states and southeastern Canada.

A twig from a giant sequoia. The leaves are very small, pointed, and shaped like triangular arrowheads.

COUNT A CLUSTER OF PINE NEEDLES

A pine tree can often be identified by the number of needles in a fascicle (cluster). It's easy to find a fascicle and then count the needles.

MATERIALS

- Your sharp eyes
- Pine twig with fascicles (clusters) of needles on it. You might find a twig or branch on the ground if there has been a lot of wind. You can also count fascicles on a small seedling or sapling pine—even if it's only one or two feet tall!

1. Look at the twig and find a cluster (fascicle) of needles. The fascicle is securely attached to the twig. Count how many needles there are.

2. Count two more fascicles, just to be sure they all have the same number of needles. (Some may have been damaged by storms or by insects.)

   Look for other pines in your area to see if they have fascicles with the same number. There are more than 20 species of pines in North America, so you might have more than one species of pine in your neighborhood.

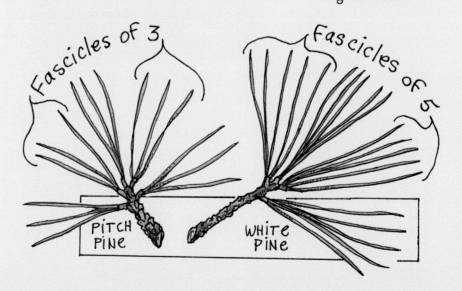

The pitch pine on the left has three needles in each fascicle. The eastern white pine on the right has five.

Larches Are Different!

Larches are different than most other members of the pine family. Pines, hemlocks, firs, and spruces are evergreen all year long, but larches turn golden yellow in the autumn—and then all the needles fall off! Larches look very colorful in the fall, but they have bare branches all winter.

Larches are also called tamaracks or hackmatacks, names originally from the Algonquian Native Americans. Three species are found in North America. The most common one grows in the northeastern United States and across much of Canada. Larches can grow about 60 feet tall and have a pointed, triangular shape. The needles are short and grow in tight clusters, or even as single needles.

The needles of tamarack trees turn gold in the fall, and then all the needles fall off. Most other members of the pine family lose only some of their needles in the autumn.

- **Ginkgo family.** These trees are native to China, where they grow wild, but they have been grown and raised in North America for a long time. Their unique, fan-shaped leaves are easy to identify. Fossil leaves of ginkgos have been found dating to the Triassic period—more than 100 million years ago!

  Although the ginkgo is a native wild tree in China, it is grown and planted throughout most of North America. The leaves turn yellow-gold in the fall. The rounded fruit has a large seed inside.

- **Palm family.** This includes the coconut palm. Palms don't have branches like other trees, but have a fountain-shaped tuft of big fronds (large leaves) at the very top. There are more than 1,000 species in this family around the world

The fan-shaped leaves of a ginkgo tree are easy to identify.

in tropical areas. Along with trees, this family also includes vines and small shrubs.

- **Willow family.** Willows are widely known for their thin, drooping branches with narrow leaves. Black willows usually grow near rivers and ponds. Pussy willows are small, shrubby members of the family. Aspens, cottonwoods, and poplars are members with rounded leaves.

- **Walnut family.** This family includes walnut, hickory, and pecan trees.

- **Laurel Family.** This family includes the sassafras, a common tree throughout most of the eastern United States. Its **range** extends south into Florida and parts of Texas, and north to Michigan and southern Maine. Historically (about 100 years ago) sassafras wood was sometimes used to make furniture and fence posts in the southern states.

- **Birch family.** Several species of birch are found across North America. Most are trees, but two species in the northern United States, in Canada, and the Arctic are very small. These dwarf birches grow close to the ground, reaching a height of only three feet.

Several species of palm trees grow in the southeast United States and in California. A young Florida royal palm like this one could grow to a height of about 80 feet.

A group of sassafras trees in fall color.

Remember: tree families are really plant families that include trees—and many members of a family might be shrubs and small plants.

- **Beech family.** Beech trees produce seeds that are eaten by deer, chipmunks, grouse, turkeys, and many other species of birds.

- **Elm family.** Elm trees are known for their spreading fountain shape or vase shape. The leaves of the American elm have a toothed edge, parallel veins, and a rough surface.

- **Oak family.** Famous and familiar for their acorns, there are more than 30 different oak tree species found in North America. Many more are shrubs.

- **Magnolia family.** Magnolia trees are native to the southern United States but have been successfully planted and grown as far north as Maine. The tulip tree is also a member of the magnolia family. A large forest tree throughout many of the eastern states, it is found as far south as Florida. The normal range also extends north to Connecticut and Massachusetts.

- **Rose family.** Roses? Yes, this plant family includes small plants like garden roses—and also strawberries and raspberries! Several trees are members of the rose family, too: apple, plum, black cherry, chokecherry, almond, and crab apple trees. Hawthorns are also included, with more than 100 species in North America.

- **Maple family.** In North America, there are more than a dozen species of maple trees. There are also many species that are shrubs. And more are found in Great Britain, Europe, and China, with a total of more than 100 species worldwide.

- **Horse chestnut family.** In North America, this includes buckeye trees. The horse chestnut is often planted as a shade tree and for its beautiful flowers. It is a native of Europe.

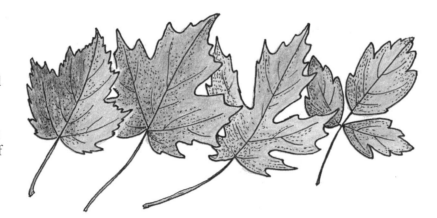

The leaves of four different species of maples. The first is a red maple, the second is a sugar maple, and the third is a silver maple. The last, a box elder maple, has a leaf divided into three leaflets.

The large cuplike flowers of the tulip tree are nearly two inches across.

- **Linden family.** Also called basswood, this family is known for its sweet-smelling flowers. In England and Europe, lindens are called lime trees, but they are not related to the lemon or lime trees that produce citrus fruit.

- **Cactus family.** A cactus doesn't look at all like the other trees listed here, but the large saguaro cactus of the desert Southwest can grow 40 to 50 feet tall. Old saguaros branch out into several upward-reaching "arms." Most cactus species are much smaller plants.

- **Dogwood family.** The flowering dogwood of the eastern states grows about 30 to 40 feet tall. It has been raised and cultivated as a landscaping tree and is commonly planted near homes and even along highways. There are smaller species of shrub-sized dogwoods—and even a woodland wildflower!

- **Tupelo family.** There are just a few species in the southeastern United States.

- **Heath family.** Rhododendrons and mountain laurels belong to the heath family. Many different cultivated varieties are raised as landscaping shrubs. The heath family also includes blueberry plants and woodland wildflowers such as trailing arbutus and wintergreen.

(*left*) The flowering dogwood tree of the eastern United States has large white petals that are called bracts. Though they are not true petals, they are quite beautiful.

(*right*) These wildflowers (called dwarf cornel or bunchberry) are members of the dogwood family, along with flowering dogwood trees. The flower stalks are only about six inches tall.

- **Olive family.** The olives you eat are part of this family, along with many different species of ash trees. Lilac and forsythia shrubs are also members.

- **More families!** There are many other plant families that include trees. The myrtle family includes the eucalyptus trees (gum trees) of Australia. There are about 500 species of eucalyptus in Australia. Although they are native to that country, many are planted in California and Florida.

  The legume family includes small plants like peas and clover, but also acacia trees, found in Hawaii and Florida, Australia, and Africa. The holly family includes the evergreen American holly tree and several shrubs.

Conifers and Deciduous Trees

Trees that have green leaves on them all year, such as pines, spruces, and hemlocks, are usually called evergreens by gardeners and nursery growers. These trees lose some of their needles in the autumn, but they are replaced by new ones. The trees still look green all year because they have lost only some of their needles. Evergreen trees like pine and spruce produce woody cones that contain seeds, so botanists called them conifers. A forest of conifers is called a coniferous forest. (A few trees from other families might remain evergreen all year, such as the American holly—but it's not a conifer.)

Trees that lose all their leaves every autumn are often called broadleaf trees, because their leaves are flat and wide. Botanists and naturalists usually call them **deciduous** (dee-SID-yuu-us) trees. The leaves of most deciduous trees turn yellow, red, or orange in the autumn, before they all fall off.

(*left*) "Champion-sized" tree species are measured by **circumference** (the distance around). But trees cut for lumber and firewood are usually measured by **diameter** (the distance across).

(*right*) The trunk of this pitch pine is 43 inches in circumference. Notice the thick, rough bark. The largest and oldest pitch pines can have a circumference of 60 to 100 inches.

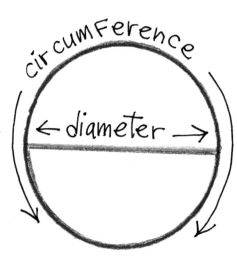

MEASURE THE CIRCUMFERENCE OF A TREE

Naturalists measure the circumference (as well as the height) of a tree to find out what is the largest (and sometimes oldest) tree in an area. You can easily measure the circumference of a tree trunk yourself.

MATERIALS

- Tape measure (the flexible tape measure used for sewing is best)
- A tree you can walk right up to
- A friend/helper

1. Have a friend hold the measuring tape in place, about 4 feet from the ground—unless you can get your arms around the tree by yourself!

2. Bring the length of measuring tape all the way around the trunk to the beginning.

3. Read the measurement in feet or inches on the tape. Now you know the circumference of that tree!

4. Find a much smaller tree or a larger tree, so you can compare sizes. After you have measured a few different trees, you will be able to estimate the circumference of other trees that have a similar size.

Hint: If you keep your tape measure in your pocket, you can measure the circumference of a tree any time!

Many of the trees in the families described here can grow very tall and have very big trunks. You can measure the **circumference** (sir-KUM-fer-ens) of a tree's trunk to find out just how big it is. Circumference is the measurement all around the trunk, about four feet from the ground.

Leaf Vein Patterns

You have already noticed the different shapes that leaves can have. There are even more patterns and designs to notice in the veins of leaves. The leaf of an American chestnut has a central vein (the midrib) that runs from the petiole to the tip, with parallel (side-by-side) veins spreading out from it. The veins on a red maple leaf don't have a central midrib. Instead, the veins spread out right from the petiole. The veins of a flowering dogwood leaf grow away from the midrib in graceful, curving arcs.

Sometimes it's easier to see the veins on a leaf if you turn it over and look at the underside. You might notice that the underside of a leaf is lighter in color than

Three different patterns of leaf veins: the straight, parallel (side-by-side) veins on an American chestnut; the branching veins of a white oak leaf that go out to the tips of the lobes; and the curving veins of a flowering dogwood.

DECORATE WITH PRESSED LEAVES

The shapes of leaves and the arrangement of their veins make interesting patterns and designs. You can use some of your pressed leaves to show these designs in an artistic way.

MATERIALS

- Pressed leaves (see the "Press Leaves to Preserve Them" activity on page 9)—smaller sizes are best to try first
- A small notebook—or two!
- Roll of clear packing tape or mailing tape (about 2 inches wide)
- Crayons or colored markers

1. Place an interesting leaf on the cover of your notebook. It's easier if you put it right in the center.

2. Cut a piece of plastic tape long enough to cover the leaf completely. Carefully press the tape over the leaf. Start with the petiole and press toward the tip. You may have to hold down the leaf with one hand.

3. Once the tape is in place, rub and press the tape over and around the leaf evenly. You might need two pieces of tape. Now you have a preserved, permanent specimen right on your notebook! You can also use crayons or markers to decorate the notebook with a colorful border, or write your name or the name of the tree on the front.

A red maple leaf was used to decorate Jane's notebook, and a small twig from an arborvitae (northern white cedar) is on Kenneth's notebook.

Name Game

Bigtooth aspen, quaking aspen (also called trembling aspen), and cottonwoods are often known by the common name *poplars* or *popples*. Here are some other common names of trees:

- A sugar maple is often called a rock maple.
- Northern white cedar is called arborvitae by gardeners and landscapers.
- Longleaf pine is also known as southern pine or yellow pine.

- American basswood is also called a linden tree. In England and Europe, basswoods are called lime trees—even though they are not related to lemon and lime citrus trees.
- Larch trees are also known as tamaracks and hackmatacks. But in California, the lodgepole pine is sometimes called a tamarack.
- Black tupelo may be called black gum or sour gum in the southern states. In New England, it is often called a pepperidge tree.

The leaves of a black tupelo, also called a pepperidge tree, turn deep red-orange in the fall.

The shagbark hickory is named for the long strips of shaggy bark that hang away from the trunk.

the top. Silver maples are known for the silvery-green undersides of their leaves.

Different Types of Bark

A white pine tree has different bark on its trunk than a black cherry tree. And a sycamore tree has very different bark than a red maple. The color, texture, and patterns on bark are different for most tree species. Bark is the tough outer covering for trees. It protects the inner part of the tree, which may still be growing. It also protects the living inner parts from storm damage or insects.

The white birch, also called paper birch, has white bark that often peels away in thin, papery pieces. White birch trees are found across the northern United States to Alaska, and across much of Canada.

Even if you can't identify a single tree in your neighborhood, take a look at the bark on the tree trunks as you walk by. You likely will see different types of bark: smooth bark, rough bark, and even bark that has a sort of pattern. You will soon develop an eye for noticing these details on other trees.

Bark has been used by Native American tribes to make small boxes and trays, birch-bark canoes, and roofs for small houses and lodges.

How Many Species of Trees Are There?

The answer is: a lot! More than 600 species of trees are native to North America. Hundreds more are non-natives—they are wild and native in other parts of world, but are raised and planted here. Eucalyptus trees are native to Australia, but they are grown and planted in California and Florida. Norway maple trees are wild and native to Scandinavia and Europe, but have been planted successfully as non-natives in North America.

Some botanists estimate that there are more than 1,000 species of shrubs and trees, both native and non-native, just in North America. Thousands more species grow in South America, Asia, Europe, Africa, and India, especially in tropical climates. Some researchers estimate that there could be 100,000 different species of trees and shrubs around the world!

BARK AND LICHENS

The trunk of a tree may be visited by insects and spiders looking for food or a place to lay eggs. A woodpecker might land on the trunk looking for those insects. There may be moss or lichens (LIKE-ins) growing on the bark. If you take a close look at a tree's bark, there might be a lot to see!

MATERIALS

- An area where you can look closely at a tree's bark
- Your sharp eyes
- Magnifying glass

1. Walk up to a tree and look at its bark. A quick look will tell you if there are holes made by wood-boring beetles or maybe by a woodpecker.

2. Look for moss or lichens. Moss usually looks green and soft. But lichens can look frilly or lacy, and many are gray-green. Lichens are very interesting to look at because of their shape and texture.

3. Use a magnifying glass to investigate the surface of the bark more closely. If the bark looks rough with deep cracks, there might be tiny insects crawling in it. You might see a small group of wingless "bark lice," or psocids (SO-sids), which feed on tiny bits of fungi and algae.

   You might also find a moth resting on the bark, especially if the tree is near a light that was left on the night before. Looking closely at bark, lichens, and moss can reveal a world of life that most people never see.

Lichens often look lacy or frilly and grow in circular "medallions" on tree bark.

A ladybug rests on a tree trunk.

23

3

....

From the Ground Up

Forests and woodlands are not just a lot of trees in one place. The underlying dirt is important to good tree growth. Nutrients are added to the dirt by a layer of decaying (rotting) leaves, twigs, and small plants. There are different **strata** (STRA-ta), or layers, of plant growth, starting right at the ground. As you look upward, other strata include: wildflowers; small ground-covering plants and shrubs; small, young trees (the **understory**); and finally all the upper branches and crowns together (the **canopy**). The different strata are visited by different birds, insects, or even mammals.

What Is a Forest?

A forest is a place where the majority of the landscape is covered by mostly mature (fully grown) trees. The trees are the dominant (main) plant forms. A forest of conifers might have mainly firs and pines growing in it. The conifers would be the dominant, or chief, type of tree. One type of deciduous forest may have mostly oaks and maples in it, while another type of deciduous forest may have mostly birches. Aspen trees are the dominant forest trees in some western states.

A forest can spread out over hundreds or thousands of acres—or many square miles! Countries around the world have large forested areas that are protected from human development and cutting for lumber.

Forested areas are also called woodlands. It doesn't make a difference whether you take a walk in a forest or a woodland—you are in a place where most of the landscape is covered by mature trees.

A **stand** of trees is a place where there are at least five acres of similar species growing together, like a small forest. A stand of maples might be five or ten acres, but it is not a whole forest. A stand can also mean an area where many trees of one species are growing together, with a different species growing around it.

Dirt First!

Trees need good soil, sunlight, and water to grow healthy roots and produce leaves and seeds. It all starts with dirt. The dirt in a woodland or forest has a lot of living things in it: fungus and mold, microscopic bacteria or other tiny organisms, and the roots of other plants. It might also contain beetles, ants, spiders, millipedes, slugs, and sow bugs, plus decaying leaves and small twigs. The insects, other small animals, and mold help to break down newly fallen leaves and twigs into smaller and smaller bits. The rotting material provides nutrients (food) for the trees.

After deciduous trees lose their leaves in autumn, a layer of fallen leaves covers the ground. The leaves dry, curl, and begin to crumble as they decay. Some forests and woodlands have a fairly deep layer of these leaves on the ground—you shuffle through them as you walk. That layer is called leaf litter. In a pine forest, the layer of old pine needles is often called pine duff. The

A mostly coniferous forest in the Sierra Nevada mountains of central California.

needles don't decay as fast as the leaves of deciduous trees, and they remain brown or golden-brown for years. They look quite pretty as you walk along a trail through the pines.

Leaves that fall on lawns and in front of buildings are usually raked up. In a forest, however, the leaf litter is important to the growing trees and to wildlife. The litter also helps prevent soil erosion, and during times of drought (when there is no rain), it helps keep the soil below from drying out.

Ground Cover Is Next

The forest floor is usually covered with small plants. In the aspen forests of Utah, beautiful blue columbine wildflowers grow in the shade of the trees. Clintonia, a member of the lily family, is found as far south as Georgia. In Newfoundland, Canada, the woods floor of a spruce forest would have delicate pink twinflower plants. And under the famous huge California redwood trees, you would see huckleberries (similar to blueberries) and ferns.

Many other flowering plants are found growing in woods and forests. Partridge-berry, goldthread, and trailing arbutus grow in forests in southern Canada and much of the United States. From

(*top left*) Pine duff on the forest floor.

(*top right*) This leaf litter contains mostly leaves from black oak and red maple trees. This photo was taken in November, after the trees dropped all their leaves.

(*left*) Shin-leaved pyrola (on the left) and wintergreen, or checkerberry (on the right), are both small flowering plants growing in woodlands. They are found across much of Canada and the northern United States.

ANIMAL LIFE AMONG WOODS FLOOR "LITTER"

You'll be amazed at the life to be found in a pile of leaves or needles!

MATERIALS

- Garden gloves or work gloves
- Area with leaf litter or pine duff
- Plastic food storage bag that can be sealed
- Your sharp eyes
- Magnifying glass

sealed bag
gloves

1. Put on your gloves and pick up a big handful of leaf litter or pine duff from the ground.

2. Stuff the leaf litter in the plastic bag and seal the bag.

3. Hold up the bag to look closely at the leaves or pine needles. Use a magnifying glass to see what is in the leaf litter.

You may have to wait a few minutes for insects, spiders, sow bugs, millipedes, or other tiny creatures to start crawling around inside the bag. They usually hold very still or curl up when they have been disturbed. The insects and other tiny animals you find in the leaf litter are there to feed, to lay eggs, or to have a safe place to rest. Even if you only find a single insect in your sample bag, you can imagine how many others are in the leaf litter of an entire forest!

4. When you are done looking at the leaf litter, dump it all back onto the ground, so the insects and other organisms can return home.

Hint: If you can't get litter from the woods, gather up some dead leaves or cut grass from the edge of a lawn or garden. You're likely to find some insects or other tiny creatures there, too.

This sow bug was found in a bag of leaf litter. Sow bugs are sometimes called roly-polies because they roll up or curl up in a round ball when frightened. They are crustaceans (not insects), along with lobsters, crabs, and shrimp!

What Is Ecology?

Ecology is the scientific investigation of animals and plants living together in the **environment**. Plants and animals living in a particular habitat are known as a community. The forest community is different in different types of forests. For example, the plants and animals in a dry desert habitat are different than the plants and animals in a wet swamp. A habitat can be a pine forest, the cold Arctic tundra, a tropical jungle, or a prairie. Each habitat supports different birds, mammals, insects, reptiles, and amphibians. **Ecologists** are scientists who study the plants and animals—and even the climate and soil—in a habitat or community.

Soil ecology is the study of the dirt, minerals, dead and decaying leaves, and twigs—and the interaction of tiny insects, spiders, fungi, mold, and microscopic life living in the dirt and leaf litter.

A forest ecologist investigates and studies the trees, smaller plants, and animals that need the forest to get their food or to make nests and dens to survive.

Winter ecology is the study of the plants and animals that live in areas where there is snow, ice, or very cold temperatures during some part of the year.

(*above*) The different levels, called strata, of a forested landscape.

(*left*) Small colonies of clintonia grow in forests and woodlands, from southeastern Canada to Georgia in the southern United States.

southeastern Canada down to the state of Georgia, you might find pink lady's slipper orchids in the woods.

Evergreen nonflowering plants, such as lycopodium (LY-ko-PO-dee-um), make small colonies along the ground. They spread by trailing root systems. Many species of mosses and ferns also cover the woods floor in forests.

Above the soil and small plants on the ground are larger plants and shrubs. Low-bush blueberry and huckleberry, which are in the heath family, often grow underneath birches and maples. They are shrubs with woody stems that grow about two or three feet tall.

Here are a few other small shrubs that grow in woodlands and forests:

- beaked hazelnut
- alder
- sheep laurel
- witch hazel (This is sometimes a small tree, growing 10 feet tall.)
- arrowwood or moosewood

Low-bush blueberry plants are woody shrubs that grow underneath black oaks and red maples.

(*left*) The pale pink flowers of trailing arbutus are often found in the woods of New England. These beautiful wildflowers are sometimes called mayflowers.

(*center*) Lycopodium, also called ground pine, are a fairly common ground cover in forests. They are a type of club moss and remain green throughout the year.

(*right*) Ferns are often found growing in deciduous woodlands of maple, oak, and birch. They also grow under the huge redwood trees in California.

Sheep laurel is a flowering woody shrub that grows at the edge of a mixed deciduous forest.

What's the Story on the Understory?

An understory of smaller trees grows beneath the large, mature trees in the forest. These are younger trees—seedlings and saplings—that grow throughout the forest. They are taller than the ground cover of ferns or wildflowers, and taller than shrubs like alder or blueberry. As big, older trees die, the younger trees have more space and sunlight to grow up. Botanists and naturalists usually include shrubs, ferns, and wildflowers when they speak of the understory.

The Canopy

Now you can look up! The upper branches and twigs of a tree make up the crown. As you walk through a summer woodland, you are under the shade of many crowns at once. The branches, twigs, and leaves make a cover over the forest called the canopy.

 TRY THIS!

ESTIMATE THE HEIGHT OF A YOUNG TREE

A young tree is called a sapling. You can make an estimate of how tall a sapling is—if you know how tall you are!

MATERIALS

- Measuring tape, or ruler and painter's tape
- Sapling

1. Find out how tall you are, using the measuring tape. Or, you can make a mark on a wall (with a piece of painter's tape) where the top of your head is. Then use a ruler to measure from that mark to the floor. (You can remove the painter's tape afterward without leaving any mark on the wall.)

2. Stand and look at a sapling. How far above your head is the top of the tree? Does it look twice as tall as you are? If you are about 4 feet tall and the tree is about twice your height, that means the tree is about 8 feet tall!

   If you know how tall you are, you can make a good estimate of the height of a young tree.

Once you have estimated the height of a few different young trees, you'll be able to make good estimates for other trees.

(*left*) Looking up into the high canopy of a woodland, with an eastern white pine in the center, surrounded by black oaks and red maples. The canopy is the crowns of all the trees together.

(*right*) A mostly coniferous forest spreads across the landscape in the Wasatch Mountains of Utah.

The canopy helps prevent heavy rain from washing away the soil below.

The upper canopy is a unique habitat: it gets the most wind and pouring rain, but it also gets the most sun. It can be a very windy place! It is a special habitat for insects and birds that need the dense mix of twigs, branches, and leaves to feed safely or to nest.

Different Types of Forests and Woodlands

Around the world, there are a variety of forests and woodlands. Here are just a few types:

- Coniferous forests. These can include species of fir, spruce, pine, and other trees that produce cones with seeds in them. People often call them evergreen forests or softwood forests.

- Boreal forests. These are mostly coniferous forests in the cold northern areas across Canada and in northern Europe and Asia. They are also called taiga (TY-ga).

- Deciduous woodlands. Deciduous woods can include a mix of oak, maple, and birch trees; beech trees; or mostly birch or aspen species. Deciduous trees are often called broadleaf trees or

START A FOREST LOGBOOK

A forest logbook is a handy way to keep a record of your observations about trees. The notes you have taken—and any drawings you make—will help you remember what you have seen.

MATERIALS

- Small notebook
- Pressed leaves (see the "Decorate with Pressed Leaves" activity on page 20) or crayon leaf rubbings (see the "Make a Crayon Rubbing of an Interesting Leaf" activity on page 8)
- Clear packing tape
- Colored pencils, pens, or crayons

1. Decorate your notebook cover with pressed leaves or crayon leaf rubbings. Use clear packing tape to stick them on.

2. Whether you are in a forest, a garden, your backyard, or a playground, write notes and make drawings of the different strata you see. Just look down. What kind of ground cover do you see? Grass, leaves, fallen branches? A lawn has a different ground cover (grass) than the weedy edge of a playground. Are there larger plants or shrubs nearby?

3. Even if you can look at only one tree, take notes about the branches and the crown. Make a drawing of the whole tree, even if you think you can't draw very well. Your notes and drawings will help you to develop observation skills—and recall the details of your observations.

4. Don't forget to put a date on what you write and draw!

hardwoods (because the logs cut from those trees are harder than those of the conifers).

- Mixed woods. In the forests of the eastern states especially, you may find conifers and deciduous trees growing together. A hilly landscape in Vermont or Maine may have white pine, black oak, and red maple all growing together.

- Rain forests. A large variety of species grow in rain forest environments, such as those in tropical areas like Hawaii, Costa Rica, South America, and the Philippines.

- Old-growth forests. Very old forests are called ancient or **old-growth forests** if most of the trees are at least 100 years old. Some old-growth forests have trees that are hundreds of years old—or more than 1,000 years old! These areas typically have not had any human activity—no home construction, no roads, and no lumber cutting or other damage caused by people. Old-growth forests are often protected by federal or state laws.

- Pine barrens. These are areas where the soil is usually dry and sandy and the trees are mostly pines. The pine barrens of New Jersey are famous for their pitch pines.

- Other forests. There are many other types of forests, including the cypress swamps of the southeastern United States; the eucalyptus forests of eastern Australia; and the cool, rainy forests of British Columbia in Canada, which are called temperate rain forests.

(*left*) The pale silver-gray trunks of a quaking aspen forest in Utah. This deciduous forest is the home of a pair of Cooper's hawks.

(*right*) A mixed woods of maple, oak, and birch just beginning to change color in early fall.

TREES THAT MAKE NOISE

Different trees make different noises. Do this activity when there is a light breeze or wind. Don't go out in really strong winds or a storm, however. You could get hurt by falling branches!

MATERIALS

- An area with trees
- Your sharp ears
- Your forest logbook and pencil

1. Listen closely for these sounds:

- Rippling sounds: Made by the leaves of quaking aspen, bigtooth aspen, or cottonwoods in a breeze. The petioles on their leaves are flat, so the leaves flap and wiggle—making a rippling sound!

- A gentle whoosh: Stand near a few black willows or weeping willows. They have long, thin, drooping branches that sway and swoosh in a wind.

- Wind in the pines: If there are pines in your area, or you can walk along a trail among pines, even a light breeze makes a pleasant "whispering" sound.

- Rattle and creak of bare branches: During the late fall and winter, when there are no leaves on deciduous trees, the branches rattle and scrape against each other. This can be a creepy, scary sound if you don't know what it is!

- Dry rustling: In late autumn and early winter, many oak trees still have clusters of dead, dry leaves on their twigs. When a breeze comes along, the dry leaves rustle and scrape against each other. This can sound like someone shuffling through the leaf litter.

2. Write down the sounds you hear in your forest logbook, along with the date and weather conditions, so you have a record of the sounds you heard.

How Deep Do Tree Roots Go?

It depends on the species of tree! Hawthorns are small trees that are often kept pruned and trimmed as shrubs. Their roots may go down only a few feet into the ground. A large sugar maple has roots that might grow six feet deep. The roots of big pines and oaks grow just five or six feet deep. Root growth depends a lot on the soil. If there is too much clay or too many stones, the roots don't grow as well as they would in loose, well-drained soil.

Most trees have somewhat shallow roots. After a hurricane or a winter storm, trees are sometimes uprooted—they are pushed over by the wind and fall to the ground with their roots in the air. The roots might look like they only went a few feet deep, even if it was a big tree. But many small roots—and tiny rootlets—were not ripped out with the rest of the larger root system and remain in the ground. Shallow roots often spread out farther than they go down! The root system of a large mature tree may grow 30 to 50 feet away from the trunk but not go very far down into the ground.

LEAVES OF THE FUTURE!

In the very late summer, or early fall, you can see what the trees have "planned" for the future—several months away!

MATERIALS

- 🌱 Your sharp eyes
- 🌱 A deciduous tree (such as a maple, oak, birch, or wild cherry) that you can get close to

1. Look closely at the twigs of the tree. There may still be leaves on it, even in early fall. But you'll notice some small buds on the ends of the twigs or near the petioles of the leaves. These buds will open up several months later.

2. Look at the twigs of different trees during the late summer and in the fall. You'll find that some species of trees have rounded buds, and others have pointy, spear-shaped buds. These leaf buds will last all through the winter—and then will open the following spring.

Do you know exactly what *you* will be doing six or seven months from now?

4

""""""""""""""""""""""

Woodland Wildlife

Forests and woodlands support a variety of wildlife. The forest community includes birds, mammals, insects, spiders, reptiles, and amphibians. The largest animals in a forest might be deer, moose, or even bears. Some of the smallest animal life you can see are springtails (also called snow fleas), which live in the leaf litter. A healthy forest ecology is a community of many species of animals and plants, living successfully in the woodland habitat.

You can look for woodland wildlife as you hike or walk in a forest—and you can usually find evidence of their activities. You can even attract some interesting forest insects!

A Grouse on the Ground

The ruffed grouse—called a partridge in some areas—is a plump woodland bird, about 16 to 18 inches long, with a tail that opens wide like a fan. It is found in much of the northern United States, south to Virginia in the east, in Alaska, and across most of Canada. It has perfect camouflage for its woodland habitat. Brown, gray, and reddish-brown feathers make it very hard to see as it hunts for food among the brown leaves and pine needles, perches in the branches of a pine, or sits on its nest.

A ruffed grouse eats mostly plant material, foraging for seeds and berries. One of its favorite foods is—of course—partridge-berry. It also eats the leaves and berries of wintergreen. The fruit of bunchberry, and even the berries of poison ivy, are other foods it eats. In the spring, a grouse also feeds on the soft parts of young ferns and the small new leaves of blackberry.

Grouse (the word is the same for a single grouse or many grouse) spend a lot of time on the ground. But in the spring, they also fly up to the tops of quaking aspens and bigtooth aspens to eat the leaf buds at the ends of twigs. They also eat the **catkins** (dangling clusters of flowers) of birch trees. In addition to berries, leaves, and seeds, grouse chicks and young grouse

(*left*) A white-tailed deer is alert to the slightest sounds in its forest habitat.

(*center*) The ruffed grouse, often called a partridge, has a group of feathers, called a crest, on the top of its head.

(*right*) The red fruits of the partridgeberry are among the berries and plants that ruffed grouse eat.

(*left*) A ruffed grouse huddles in leaf litter. The camouflage pattern of its feathers makes it very hard to see.

(*right*) A goshawk zooms in through the bare branches of a winter forest, hunting for grouse, squirrels, and rabbits.

eat beetles, ants, caterpillars, spiders, and even slugs.

Grouse are considered a game bird in many states and are hunted by sportsmen in the fall. Grouse are also hunted by goshawks, large forest hawks that have short wings for flying swiftly through woodlands. Surviving in the forest means being able to remain hidden while searching for food on the ground or roosting safely. Having camouflage coloration is important. So is sitting very still.

A female grouse sitting on its nest on the ground is hard to see. But a roaming dog—perhaps allowed to run free, away from a hiking trail—is a deadly danger! It can smell a grouse and rush up and kill it before anyone can stop it. A grouse must be constantly alert to strange sounds.

During the winter, grouse must also survive temperatures that are below freezing, as well as sleet storms and snowstorms. They sometimes burrow partway into soft snow, huddling for protection against cold and wind.

Mice and Voles, Shrews and Moles (and More)

The grouse is not alone as it searches for food on the ground. Small mammals, all just a few inches in length, also are foraging on the woods floor. Across North America, many different species of mice look for seeds, berries, nuts, and insects, which they find on or near the ground.

Voles look somewhat like mice but have very short ears and smaller eyes. Voles usually hunt for food just under the layer of leaf litter. They look for plant roots and bulbs, young shoots and sprouts, and seeds.

Shrews are about the same size as a mouse but have a longer, pointier nose. Shrews are famous for their big appetites. They constantly hunt, looking for beetles, grubs, worms, spiders, and even centipedes. There are more than 20 different species of shrews in North America.

Moles burrow into the ground easily using their wide front paws and claws, which are adapted for digging. They also

YOU ARE A GROUSE—ON THE ALERT

Imagine what it would be like to live in the forest and be alert to all the sounds around you.

MATERIALS

- Your imagination
- Your sharp attention to details
- A few trees to look at (pines or other conifers are best)
- Forest logbook and pencil

1. Stand outside where you have a good view of pines (or imagine that you are in a forest).

2. Think about getting something to eat. Since you're a grouse, you would really like a few ripe red partridgeberries. A young grouse also would like to have a few beetles.

3. Imagine that you have a thick stand of trees to roost in safely.

4. Pay sharp attention to the noises you hear around you. Which sounds are natural?

(The wind, leaves rustling, a crow calling, or a cicada [a large insect] buzzing high in the treetops.) Which sounds are not natural, or are man-made? (A dog barking, a truck zooming by, or a plane overhead.) Which sounds are safe to be near? Which could be a danger? Hint: Use your forest logbook to write down your ideas of what it might be like to live in the forest.

A grouse has to be able to see and hear danger, and be alert to all of its surroundings—just as you need to be alert crossing the street!

forage just under the leaf litter. They hunt for beetles and other insects, grubs, and earthworms.

During the cold winter months, many of these small mammals are quite active, burrowing and tunneling under the snow. Throughout the year, small woodland mammals are the natural prey of native predators such as hawks, owls, and foxes.

But that's not all—chipmunks, ground squirrels, red squirrels, gray squirrels, and flying squirrels also are common residents

From top to bottom: a mouse, a vole, a shrew, and a mole. All can be found in forests and woodlands.

40

of the forest. Larger forest mammals include foxes, raccoons, rabbits, hares, porcupines, and bobcats. Still larger are moose and deer, elk in the western states, and bears. The surrounding forest trees provide habitat for these animals to find food, to remain hidden, to rest, or to make a nest or den.

Moths in the Forest

You might not think that moths are beautiful, but many species are colorful or have interesting patterns. One species, called the white underwing, is just black and white, but it is very well camouflaged when resting on tree bark. The **larva** (caterpillar) feeds on the leaves of willow and aspen trees.

The pale green luna moth is a colorful species found in the eastern half of the United States. It has a wingspan of about four inches and long graceful "tails" on its hindwings. Its larvae eat the leaves of oak, birch, hickory, and other woodland trees.

The larvae of underwing and luna moths eat the leaves of deciduous forest trees. They do not damage whole trees or stands of trees, however, because they are not abundant (meaning they are not very common). But many other species of forest moths are so abundant that the larvae can be quite destructive.

(*top left*) Porcupines are fairly common in forests throughout most of Canada, the northeast United States, the western states, and Alaska. But an albino porcupine, shown here, is a rare sight!

(*top right*) A white underwing moth is hard to spot on the trunk of a white birch tree.

(*left*) A luna moth rests on the bark of a white pine tree.

Gypsy moth larvae and "tent caterpillars" (the larvae of smaller, brown moths) can completely defoliate trees. That means they eat all the leaves, so the trees look bare! Every year, **entomologists** (scientists who study insects) are on the alert for destructive species of moths. They need to inform foresters, state parks, landscapers, and the public about the insects to watch for, in case there is an infestation (an abundance of destructive species).

Look! Up in the Trees!

Up in the forest canopy, there are small moths, beetles, aphids, caterpillars, and spiders crawling around on the twigs and leaves. These are the food of warblers, small birds that find a feast on the upper branches of the forest. Because they feed mostly on insects, they have to migrate (fly southward) once the weather becomes too cold to hunt for food. Many warblers are quite colorful, and many have memorable songs. A good example is the black-throated green warbler. It has a song that sounds like an enthusiastic *zee-zee-zoo-ZEET*! The black-and-white warbler calls out *we see, we see, we see*.

More than 30 species of warblers are found across North America. For many bird-watchers, the first few weeks of May are a special time to watch for the returning warblers.

Warblers are joined by flycatchers, colorful tanagers, and several species of vireos in their hunt for insects and spiders.

Larvae on the Leaves

Several species of butterflies need trees for survival also. The larvae of tiger swallowtail butterflies eat the leaves of black cherry. White admiral butterflies are often seen fluttering along woodland trails. Their caterpillars feed on birch and aspen leaves. The larvae of mourning cloaks eat elm leaves, usually feeding together in small groups. The caterpillars of the question mark butterfly (yes, that's its real name!) feed on elm leaves also. None of these species cause any real damage to trees as they eat, because they are not abundant.

(*left*) A black-and-white warbler spends a lot of time in the treetops, hunting for insects.

(*right*) Red-eyed vireos are common birds of the treetops, where they feed on insects.

"PAINT" BARK WITH A RECIPE TO ATTRACT WOODLAND MOTHS

Moths and other woodland insects will come to eat at a sweet mixture "painted" or smeared on tree bark. They will fly to the tree during the night, and many will remain, resting on the tree trunk until the morning. Entomologists call this method of attracting insects sugaring.

MATERIALS

- Small cup (a paper cup that can be recycled is good)
- 5 or 6 heaping teaspoons brown sugar
- 1 or 2 teaspoons fruit juice, such as apple juice or orange juice
- A tree that you can visit in the morning and then again in the evening or the next morning. (You should get permission to use a tree at your school or playground.)
- Old paintbrush, or some folded-up paper towels
- Forest logbook and pencil

1. In a cup, mix the brown sugar with just enough juice to make a thick mixture. (You can also add a chunk of ripe mashed-up banana. Or just use molasses, by itself).

2. Choose a tree that is near your house, or one that you can visit easily.

3. Use an old paintbrush or paper towels to smear the mixture on a tree trunk. Paint it on at eye level so it will be easy for you to look at.

4. Visit the tree again to inspect the bark in the evening (if you can do it safely) or the next morning.

The trunk of a red maple tree is being painted with a thick brown-sugar mixture to attract moths.

5. Be sure to write down what you see—and when—in your forest logbook.

If you try this sugaring experiment in the summer, try it again in the fall, when there might be different species, or more species, in the area.

43

It might seem that it's safe for these birds to look for food in the treetops, but small birds are hunted by hawks. The birds have to be on the alert at all times while they feed.

Once the nesting season has started, other dangers arise. Some forest songbirds nest right on the ground. Black-and-white warblers, ovenbirds, and veeries all make nests on the woods floor. A raccoon might come along at night and eat the eggs from a nest. A stray housecat roaming loose in the woods can destroy an entire nest of fledglings in just a few minutes.

It's a (Quiet) Winter Wonderland!

The snowy forest in winter can seem deserted and empty. Birds, such as warblers, that eat mostly insects have all migrated south. Some mammals, such as chipmunks, are hibernating. Snakes, frogs, turtles, and toads are also hibernating. It's a quiet place. But some of the wildlife are still active and busy. Grouse need to find thick stands of conifers to rest in, out of the wind and cold. Nuthatches and chickadees look for birch seeds and pine seeds. Woodpeckers can still find the grubs of beetles under rotting bark and dead branches.

On the surface of the snow, you might see a patch of light gray, or a pale shadow. Look very closely—it's moving! The gray shadow is actually thousands of springtails, which are also called snow fleas. But they aren't fleas. In fact, springtails aren't insects at all. Although they were once classified as insects, they are now in their own special group. There are more than 1,000 species of springtails worldwide!

Springtails are harmless, feeding on decaying vegetation. They gather together

(*left*) Frogs, toads, and other amphibians hibernate during the winter. This is a wood frog, common in woodlands in Alaska, southern Canada, and much of the United States.

(*right*) A flying squirrel clings to the trunk of a pine tree. This photo was taken around 10 o'clock at night, with a flash.

SPRINGTAILS IN THE SNOW

This activity is best done during a mild day at the end of winter.

MATERIALS

- Your sharp eyes
- A snowy area in the woods or near a tree

1. Look for a gray or "dirty" patch of snow in the woods, or find a place where there's some snow near the base of a tree.

2. Crouch down close to the snow. Look for tiny dark dots popping around. Those are the springtails. Don't worry

A magnified view of two springtails, also called snow fleas.

if the springtails jump onto your boots or clothes. They are harmless and will soon pop away again.

You can also find springtails late in the fall or early in the spring. They will be moving along across the leaf litter. If you stand and watch, you can see the entire herd of them making (slow) progress across the woods floor.

Day and Night

If you were to take a daytime walk in a winter woodland, it might seem very quiet at first. But if you listen carefully, you might hear some interesting sounds. A nuthatch could be tapping on a branch to flip away loose bark as it hunts for insects or insect eggs. You might hear a woodpecker's cackling laugh. You also might hear the constant rustle of dry leaves, still attached to the twigs of beech trees and oaks.

At night a pair of flying squirrels might be gliding from branch to branch, in search of seeds. These small nocturnal squirrels make high chirping noises, like a bird. And a great horned owl might be hooting as it hunts for mice, voles, and shrews. Raccoons forage on mild nights, chattering away, especially when a family group is together.

in a huge group like a moving shadow when they have to travel to a new part of the woods floor. They hop and spring forward, moving over the snow, stumps and logs, and fallen branches. Springtails are very small, about the size of these dashes: - - - - - - - . A magnifying glass would show you that they look velvety and chubby—and kind of cute! It's very difficult to catch just one or two for a close look, because they pop away immediately. But if you just crouch down and watch closely, you can see hundreds at a time.

Wildlife on the Move

Wherever there is snow on the ground in forests and woodlands, you might find evidence of animal activity. Tracks in the snow are an easy way to find out which animals live there—and what they have been doing. Deer, grouse, foxes, rabbits, and hares all need to move around during the winter months.

Squirrels also run around in the snow, digging up acorns. Grouse leave star-shaped tracks in the snow, one in front of the other. A rabbit or hare leaves tracks showing hind feet that are much longer than the front feet. A deer has pointed oval tracks. A moose leaves very large tracks!

What Are the Tallest Trees?

Across North America, several species of trees grow about 100 feet tall. White oak, Shumard oak, sugar maple, and red pine all can grow to that height. American elm, tulip tree, western white pine, and sweet gum often grow a bit higher than 100 feet. Ponderosa pine and Sitka spruce trees can reach 200 feet. Douglas fir can grow more than 200 feet. The tallest trees are the famous giant sequoias and the coast redwoods, growing on the West Coast of North America. Many giant sequoias are 250 feet tall. Hyperion, a coast redwood in California, is more than 370 feet tall!

The American Forests organization keeps a list of the largest trees across the United States. The list, called American Forests Champion Trees, is updated every few years.

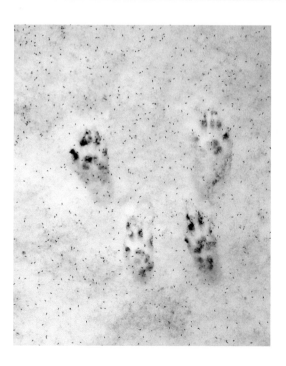

(*left*) The tracks of a gray squirrel in the snow.

(*above*) Red squirrels are active throughout the winter. When disturbed or alarmed, they make high chirps and squeaks like those of birds.

TRACKS IN THE SNOW

Whenever there is snow on the ground, your chances of finding the tracks of wildlife are good.

MATERIALS

- Your sharp eyes
- Any snowy area, even a patch of snow (a thin new covering of snow is best; an open area or near some trees is a good place to look)
- Forest logbook and pencil

1. Look for tracks near the base of a tree. You might find tracks from a squirrel coming down the trunk and going away into the woods.

2. Look at the snow near conifers such as pines, spruce, or hemlocks. You may see a single-file line of tracks made by a grouse after it has left the shelter of the trees.

3. You might see the tracks of a deer near a woodland trail.

4. Make drawings in your forest logbook of any tracks you find. You may not be able to identify them right away, but you can find out what they are another time. Don't forget to write the date and place!

If you cannot visit a woodland, look for tracks in a snowy city park. You are likely to see the tracks of squirrels, mourning doves, and crows—or tracks of ducks if there is a pond. Even along a sidewalk, you might see tracks of pigeons and sparrows. These observations will give you experience for noticing other tracks later.

mark of short hind Toe

The tracks of a ruffed grouse in snow, about one-half life-size. Each footprint is about two inches long. The hind toe is very short, and leaves only a tiny mark.

5

,,,,,,,,,,,,,,,,,,,,,,,,

It's Dead . . .
No, It's Alive!

Some people may think that a dead tree or a rotting log is ugly and useless. But dead trees, fallen logs, and rotting stumps are very important to the healthy ecology of woodlands and forests. Dead and decaying trees provide food, shelter, and nesting sites for a variety of wildlife. They even offer a place for wildlife to communicate! And small plants such as mosses and wintergreen thrive on decaying stumps.

Life in a Dead Tree: The Hole Story

An upright, standing dead tree is frequently a home for birds. Different species of wood-peckers, flycatchers, chickadees, titmice, and nuthatches all make their nests in the holes and hollows of dead trees. Screech owls and tree swallows nest in the hollows of trees.

The first birds to use a decaying or dead tree are often large woodpeckers, which can easily use their beaks to peck and hack their way into soft, rotting wood. They may have already pecked into the bark and wood to eat beetles, grubs, or carpenter ants. Woodpeckers can spend days excavating a hole to make it bigger or deeper, to use as a nest. They may even have to work on a few different standing trees before they find one that is just right. If the hole can't be made big enough, or is abandoned for a better site, a chickadee or nuthatch may use it instead. The smaller birds can continue to excavate the hole further, taking out beakful after beakful of wood chips.

Small mammals also use dead trees for their dens. Flying squirrels are found across

(left) This standing dead tree has holes made by woodpeckers looking for insects.

(center) A pileated woodpecker looks for insects—especially ants—in a dead paper birch. The bird is about the size of a crow.

(right) Notice the head of a downy wood-pecker, looking out from its nest hole toward the bottom of the photo. Downies are small, only about six to seven inches long.

most of Canada, the eastern half of the United States, and parts of the western states. They make dens in old woodpecker nests. During the coldest winter days, several squirrels may huddle together in one den to keep warm.

Not Standing Tall at All

A standing, upright dead tree gets shorter and shorter as it decays. It loses branches and the very top of its crown. Wind, storms, ice, and heavy snow all break off parts of the tree. What is left is often just a **snag**—an upright section of a hollow, rotting trunk. Snags that have been standing for several years usually have lost all or most of their bark and have a very light brown color. Even short snags are attractive to chickadees and nuthatches, which often nest only 5 to 10 feet from the ground. Chipmunks and mice usually nest in burrows, but they also use snags as hiding places or lookouts.

(*top left*) Screech owls nest in the hollow parts of a decaying tree, or in tree holes that have been hollowed out by other birds. (They can't peck or hack away the wood themselves.) Screech owls live in the southern New England states southward to Florida and Texas. The one shown here is reddish, but there is also a gray color phase.

(*above*) This snag has several holes in it, made by woodpeckers.

(*left*) An eastern chipmunk sits atop the hollow stump of a balsam fir, which it uses as a hideout.

(*right*) A decaying mossy log attracts insects, toads, and woodpeckers.

(*bottom left*) This redback salamander is just over three inches long. It crawls under rotten logs and stumps to make a nest.

(*bottom right*) An American toad hunts for insects, worms, and spiders during the night, but hides under decaying logs or stumps during the day.

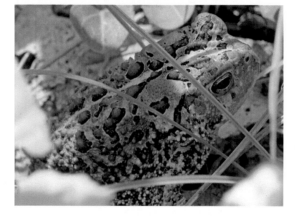

Bats are other mammals that use holes in standing trees. Many species of bats use caves to nest and roost in, but some use a hollow tree or a big crack in a dead tree to roost in during the day.

Life in a Log

After a tree has fallen over, it is still important to wildlife—big and small. As it lies on the ground, it is likely to be visited by two species of woodpeckers: the pileated and the hairy. Although both species look for insects higher up in the trees, they frequently peck apart bark and wood right on the ground.

A variety of insects, spiders, millipedes, sow bugs, and even slugs will use the log as a home, or to find food. Ants and termites will munch tunnels into the bark and wood. All of these tiny animals are food for birds and for small mammals like mice, voles, shrews, and moles.

A log that is decaying on the ground gets soft and often stays wet after a rain. Some naturalists call this condition red rot because the log is dark red-brown and stays damp. Mosses and lichens start to grow over it. Small animals are able to dig in the soil under the edge of the log and find a safe place to hide or nest. Toads can burrow under the edge of the log, and salamanders can also crawl under the rotting bark or under the log.

Meet the Beetles

Many species of beetles are attracted to dead trees, snags, and fallen logs. Some wood-boring beetles are small. But one family, called long-horned beetles, are more than an inch long, with antennae that are as long as—or longer than—their bodies! Adults lay their eggs under the bark or in the wood, which they have chewed into. The beetle larvae (grubs) grow and develop in the wood, munching long tunnels as they crawl around. If you listen carefully as you stand next to a log, you might even hear the big grubs of long-horned beetles munching away. In recent years, there has been much concern over the Asian long-horned beetle (a species native to China and Korea), which is very destructive to trees in North America. As they mature, the grubs of many species of beetles munch their way out of the wood, leaving tiny piles of "sawdust" and holes where they have emerged.

Did You Hear That?

A dead tree or log can be a kind of forest communication center. Hairy woodpeckers, common throughout most of the United States and Canada, use dead trees to announce their territory or attract mates. They tap their beaks rapidly on the side of a dead tree or on a large hollow branch. They

Picture-Perfect?

A woodland or forest may look like a beautiful landscape of tall, mature trees, but it's not quite picture-perfect. A closer inspection usually reveals that some trees have dead branches or that a few are dead standing trees. You may notice that there are many decaying logs, branches, or twigs lying on the ground. Some northern coniferous forests have so many fallen branches and twigs on the woods floor that it's almost impossible to walk around, unless there's a trail.

It is normal for a woodland to have a variety of dead and decaying trees, snags, logs, and branches. All that rotting wood provides food, homes, and shelter for a variety of birds, mammals, reptiles, and amphibians. The decaying trees and branches are an important part of a healthy forest ecology—a successful community of animals and plants living together.

(*left*) This wood-boring, or long-horned, beetle is a bit more than one inch long, with antennae about the same length.

(*right*) Large colonies of ants are frequently found in dead trees, rotten logs, and old stumps. The winged ants are males, swarming along with workers.

EVIDENCE OF HOLE MAKERS AND HOLE USERS

Even the trees in a city park may not be picture-perfect. Use your observation skills to decide whether insects, birds, or mammals have been working in the trees.

MATERIALS

- Your sharp eyes
- A few trees to look at—living or dead—in a park or along a street. Or you can use a log lying on the ground.

1. Look for chips of wood, splinters of wood, or flakes of bark on the ground at the base of a tree. These are most likely the work of a woodpecker looking for beetles, grubs, or ants.

2. Is there "sawdust" under the edge of a log? That could mean that beetles or grubs have been munching into the bark or wood. Small round holes (a quarter-inch across, or less) could mean that wood-boring beetles have emerged.

Look for holes in a dead tree and try to decide whether birds or insects made them.

3. Compare hole shapes and sizes. A rounded hole just over an inch across might be the entrance to the nest of a chickadee or nuthatch. A large rectangular hole (doorway-shaped) is the work of a pileated woodpecker pecking into the wood for carpenter ants. A hole chewed all around the edge might be the entrance to a red squirrel nest or flying squirrel nest. The squirrels chew around the entrance to make it bigger.

As you look at more evidence, you will gain the experience to judge whether birds, insects, or mammals have been at work.

tap for a few seconds at a time and repeat the tapping again and again. They peck so rapidly that you can't count the individual taps. This rapid tapping is called drumming. Both males and females drum. The drumming is usually heard toward the end of winter and through the spring. Other woodpeckers that drum include the downy woodpecker, yellow-bellied sapsucker, red-bellied woodpecker, and the larger crow-sized pileated. The pileated woodpecker makes a slower, deeper series of taps than the others.

Fallen logs are used by male ruffed grouse for a different kind of drumming. In spring and summer, the male grouse jumps up on a log and starts to beat his wings sharply downward. He begins slowly and then whisks his wings downward faster and faster, while standing in place. As his wings are sharply whisked up and down on the log, they make a deep *whump, whump, whump* sound. The *whumps* get faster and faster until his wings are a blur—and then he stops. The grouse is announcing his territory (or advertising for a mate), just like the woodpeckers.

Watch That Stump!

When a tree has been cut down for firewood or for lumber, a flat-topped stump is usually left. A more ragged, splintered stump is left when a tree falls over in a storm. It can take years for a stump to rot and decay to the ground. Beetle grubs, ants, and woodpeckers are all active munching or chipping away at it. Mammals are also at work. Skunks may scratch and dig at the stump, looking for grubs or other insects. Mice burrow under the edge of the stump, among the roots, to make their nests.

Rain, snow, and ice make the wood soft and damp and help to speed up the decay. It becomes easier for insects to lay their eggs in the soft wood and for the larvae to develop. Mold, mushrooms, and fungus also grow on stumps. Some are quite colorful and interesting. A common fungus is called turkey tail because the cluster fans out like the open tail of a turkey.

If you could watch an individual stump month after month, you might see a wood frog, toad, or small ring-necked snake wriggle among the roots around the stump. Salamanders may crawl across the stump, looking for small insects. As the months go by, moss, mold, fungus, and mushrooms might start to appear. Woodland wildflowers such as wintergreen or partridgeberry might start to grow at the sides or edge of an old stump.

Just like a standing dead tree, or a broken snag, a stump isn't simply a dead

(*top left*) A female hairy woodpecker rests on a red maple.

(*above*) A cluster of turkey tail fungus grows on a decaying stump.

(*left*) It takes several years for moss to cover a stump. This mossy stump has colorful mushrooms growing on it.

thing—it's alive with the activity of animals, and even other plants!

How Old Was That Tree?

If a tree has been freshly cut for firewood or to clear away a building lot or road, it will have a flat surface that may show its growth rings (also called **annual rings**). The rings might not be very clear, but sometimes you can see most of them. A piece of cut wood that has been sanded very smooth shows the rings best. Each ring is made by the inner layer of wood that was formed during each growing season. Some years have better growing seasons than others. A summer of drought may prevent the tree from growing very much. You may see thick or thin growth rings depending on the amount of rain that fell each year. You can count about how old the tree was by counting each ring. Each ring usually equals a year of growth.

Crows frequently use dead pines as watchtowers to keep an eye on their territory or look for food.

Please Do Not Disturb

Many different animals live under logs or pieces of logs lying on the ground. Sow bugs, millipedes, beetles, spiders, toads, snakes, and salamanders all live under (or can crawl under) decaying logs or stumps. You might be tempted to turn over or lift rotting logs. While it might look easy to move them or kick them apart, please don't try it. In some parts of North America, there could be a poisonous snake lying under the log! Also, it would be a tragedy to lift up a piece of old log and expose a nesting salamander—and hurt her or crush her eggs when you set the log back down. It's best to simply observe without disrupting the homes of small woodland animals. And it's safer.

A redback salamander guards her eggs under a piece of decaying stump. Some species of salamanders lay their eggs in ponds and streams, but others lay their eggs on land.

COUNT TREE RINGS

Find out how old a tree was when it was cut down by counting its rings.

MATERIALS

- The photo below

1. Start from the center. Count the growth rings to find out how many years old this tree was when it was cut down. Each ring equals one year (one growing season). You might not be able to count every single ring, but you should be able to count most of them.

2. Now that you've counted most of the rings, you can estimate about how many years old this pine tree was when it was cut to build a log cabin.

   A different tree with the same circumference (or diameter) may have fewer rings—or more—depending on how good the growing seasons were from year to year.

The annual rings are easy to see on the end of this old pine log. The log is at the corner of a log cabin and has a diameter of about nine inches.

A cut piece of red oak that has been sanded smooth. The darker wood in the center is called the **heartwood**. The pale wood outside the heartwood is called **sapwood**. Some species of trees do not show a color difference between the heartwood and sapwood.

DRAW IT—ADD TO YOUR FOREST LOGBOOK

List and report—or draw—in your logbook what you have seen on a dead tree, snag, or stump.

MATERIALS

- Your forest logbook
- Colored pencils, pens, or crayons

1. Make a list of what you have seen on a dead tree, snag, or stump. Have you seen woodpeckers use the tree? Or a crow use it as a lookout?

2. Try to divide your notes into three lists: a list for trees, a list for snags, and a list for stumps.

3. Make a drawing of something special you have seen—for example, a salamander, a colorful fungus, a big beetle, ants, or a woodpecker. Don't worry if you can't draw well. Your drawing is an important addition to your list. It will help you remember exactly what you observed.

Remember to write down the date and place where you saw something interesting. You might not be able to revisit some of the trees you have seen, so keeping a written list or drawing (with dates and places) can be important.

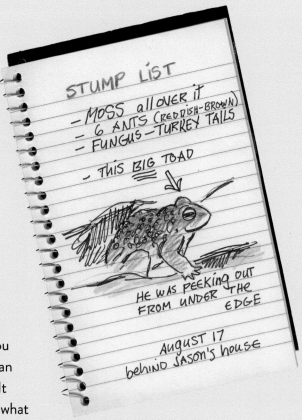

Lightning Strikes a Tree

Most woodland trees have a life span of 60 to 80 years. That's because they may be severely damaged or killed by storms. Hurricanes, flooding, tornadoes, mudslides, and ice storms can kill trees. The trees may be completely uprooted, broken, or lose so many big branches that they cannot recover. Wildfires can destroy hundreds and even thousands of acres of forests. Long periods of drought (no rain, or very little rain) can also kill trees. An infestation of some types of insects can damage or kill a tree. The emerald ash borer, a green beetle about one-half inch long, has been very destructive to trees in southeastern Canada and the eastern United States.

Lightning is an impressive killer of trees. It can strike a tree in the middle of a dense woodland or a tree standing alone in the open. It can strike a deciduous tree or a conifer. Sometimes a tree remains standing for years after it has been struck, losing its bark and slowly decaying. A direct strike often sends huge splinters flying off the trunk. The splinters are several feet long, like big spears or javelins. Sometimes the tree falls over right after the lightning strike, cracking away from the base and

How Long Can Trees Live?

Many trees in cities, in parks, and on farms can live much longer than some forest trees can. That's because they were planted to provide shade or to create a beautiful green space. The trees are taken care of by city workers, **arborists** (tree care specialists), or park rangers. They are watered if there is a drought, trimmed or pruned if necessary, fertilized, and sprayed against insects. Some towns and communities even have a tree commissioner who makes sure that "street trees" get the care they need.

Some trees have become famous for their age. The Wye Oak in Wye Mills, Maryland—a white oak about 460 years old—fell over in a thunderstorm in 2002. Hemlock and red spruce stands in Maine have been estimated to be about 300 years old. The mature redwoods of California are about 400 to 500 years old, and at least one is estimated to be more than 2,000 years old. Some western junipers are about 2,000 to 3,000 years old, and General Sherman is a giant sequoia that has lived more than 3,000 years. In Chile (South America) some araucaria trees are about 1,000 years old. The oldest trees in North America are bristlecone pines in California and the western states. Some specimens are more than 4,000 years old! Recently, researchers in Sweden believe they have found the oldest tree in the world—a spruce on a mountain in central Sweden that has been alive for about 9,500 years.

leaving a jagged stump. Lightning can also start forest fires that spread over many acres. Dead trees are like time machines, telling a story of the past: of storms, lightning, drought, or insect infestations. A forest tree that has lived for 60 to 80 years has lived through many different events!

This eastern white pine was struck by lightning during a late summer thunderstorm. The trunk has fallen aside, leaving a jagged stump.

6

'''''''''''''''''''''''

It's Nuts!
Food for Animals

Trees provide homes for a large variety of woodland wildlife. They also offer safe roosting and resting places. And the seeds, nuts, and berries from trees supply food for many animals. Many different species of birds feed on tree seeds and berries. Squirrels, deer, mice, and other mammals eat nuts, acorns, and seeds. Street trees in towns and cities offer seeds too. Maple, ash, oak, hawthorn, pine, and spruce trees are just a few of the types of trees that are important to wildlife. A healthy woodland ecology (the successful "community" of animals and plants living together in their environment) includes the food that is available from trees.

Trees also are a source of food for people. Apples, plums, pears, almonds, walnuts, and pecans are all grown in orchards or on plantations—and are just a sample of the food we get from trees for ourselves.

Go Bananas!

Many people like bananas, but we may not think about where they come from. Banana trees are native (growing wild) in Asia, but they are planted and grown in California and Louisiana. The bananas you buy in a store are usually grown in Guatemala, in Central America, or Ecuador, in South America. When you buy bananas in a grocery store, look closely at the small sticker or label on a bunch—it will show you where they were grown.

Banana trees are not large; they grow only about 20 feet tall. Although you can see lots of tiny seeds when you bite into a banana, the trees are never grown from these seeds. Instead, shoots (like small, thin trunks) grow from the base of a "mother tree," then are pulled away and planted separately. The place where the trees are raised is called a plantation.

Just Nuts

Walnut, hickory, and pecan trees all belong to the walnut family. Most species in the walnut family grow in the eastern and central United States. All of them produce edible nuts inside a hard shell and covered by a tough husk, or hull. If you have ever tried to crack open a walnut or pecan, you know you need a nutcracker to open the shell and get at the nut inside. (You can buy shelled pecans or walnuts in a store, which have already had the outer husks and shells removed.) Squirrels, chipmunks, and mice can chew through the husk and shell to eat the nutmeat inside.

The seeds of beech trees are often called beechnuts or beech mast. Beechnuts are three-sided seeds covered by a husk that has little curved spines all over it. The seeds are eaten by blue jays, grouse, porcupines, red squirrels, gray squirrels, and chipmunks. Cultivated beech trees are sometimes planted for shade. The beech family

The green outer husks of shagbark hickory nuts are thick, covering the hard shell and nuts inside. The husks (hulls) will slowly dry and become much thinner.

The nuts on the branches of a black walnut tree are covered by a greenish husk. Walnut trees usually grow 60 to 80 feet tall.

(left) The seeds of a European beech (in the foreground) are three-sided. The husks have opened, and it is easy to see their rough outer texture. The European beech is often planted in the United States as a shade tree. The seeds are quite similar to those of the native American beech.

(right) The acorns of a white oak are rounded, with a point at one end.

also includes the American chestnut tree, another species that produces edible nuts for wildlife.

Oaks and Acorns

At least 40 different species of oaks are found across North America. Some, like the white oak, have leaves with rounded lobes. Other species have leaves that are oval shaped or have wavy edges.

All oaks produce acorns. Acorns can be rounded or oval, are pointed at one end, and have a cap at the other end where they are attached to a twig. The caps can be flat or cup-shaped. Acorns are greenish at first but turn brown as they dry. If you could crush an acorn's outer shell or peel it open, you would find the edible part inside. Ruffed grouse, wood ducks, and blue jays all eat acorns. Blue jays are often noted for "planting a forest," because they store acorns for later use by poking them into soft ground—and then they forget (or don't use) some of them. The acorns sprout and grow new oak trees! In California and the extreme Southwest, acorn woodpeckers are famous for storing acorns. They make holes in a tree trunk and then poke the acorns into the holes to store them for winter. Wild turkeys can swallow small acorns whole! Deer, squirrels, and chipmunks also eat acorns.

The acorns of black oaks and red oaks don't ripen until the second year. So some years seem to be better "acorn years" than others, and in the good years squirrels run around frantically collecting them.

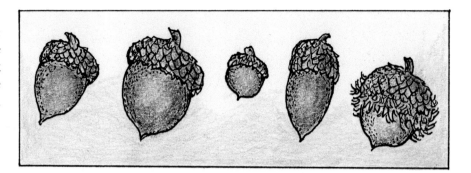

From left to right: the acorn of a white oak, red oak, pin oak (the smallest), live oak, and bur oak, which has an interesting fringed cap.

Blue jays eat oak acorns and even hide them for later use, poking them under the leaf litter or in soft ground. They also eat beech nuts and the fruit of chokecherry and serviceberry trees.

Nuts? Seeds? Parachutes??

The word that botanists and naturalists use for seeds, nuts, and berries that come from trees is—*fruit!* We typically think of fruit as apples, pears, oranges, and such. And we usually use the word *nut* for such things as hard-shelled pecans and walnuts. But to a scientist, they are all the fruit of the trees.

It can be confusing. The fruit of a pecan, walnut, or hickory tree has an outer husk and then an inner hard shell, with the edible fruit—or what we commonly call a nut—inside. The edible part is sometimes called the kernel, or nutmeat.

But there are even more types of tree fruit. The fruits of maples and ashes are called **samaras** (sa-MAR-ahs). The samaras have a seed at one end and a flat papery "wing" attached. The berries of mulberry trees and cherry trees are fruit also. The fruits of birch trees are called catkins. Catkins are dangling clusters, about one to two inches long. Male catkin flowers contain **pollen**—tiny grains produced by the male parts of plants. Female catkin clusters develop seeds. The fruits of many species in the willow family are seeds with a fluffy, cottony "parachute" attached. Aspens and cottonwoods are famous for the fluffy, silky hairs that spread out and allow each seed to float on a breeze and drift away from the tree.

Winged Seeds

The fruits of ash trees are long and narrow, and grouped in pairs or clusters. Each seed has a thin papery blade or "wing" at one end. The entire fruit is called a samara (sa-MAR-ah). Several species of ash trees are found in North America, and the seeds from the samaras are eaten by bobwhite quail, pine grosbeaks, and purple finches.

Maple trees also have fruits that are called samaras. A flat wing is attached to each paired seed. Red maple trees have samaras that are reddish at first and then dry to greenish-brown. Maple samaras are eaten by evening grosbeaks, which use their strong, thick beaks to munch away the "wing" and then open the covering of the seed. The samaras of sugar maples and Norway maples are mostly green when fresh. As the samaras dry, the pair of seeds often split apart. Maple samaras are often called helicopters because they spin around and around as they fall to the ground.

Conifers and Cones

Pines, spruces, redwoods, sequoias, and several other types of trees bear woody cones made up of curving scales. At the base of each scale are small rounded seeds with a flat papery "wing." The seeds of conifers are small. Most conifers are called evergreens, because they don't lose all their leaves each autumn. (The leaves of larch trees, however, turn golden brown and completely fall off.) Seeds from the cones of conifers are eaten by pine siskins, nuthatches, chickadees, and crossbills. These birds can pry out the seeds from the cones that are hanging on the trees.

Red squirrels and chipmunks look for pinecones that have fallen to the ground. They sit and take apart the cones, leaving a telltale pile of cone scales. You may see a pile of cone scales on a stump or rock,

The gray squirrel is a common sight in forests and even city parks, where it scampers around looking for acorns, hickory nuts, and beechnuts.

(*above*) Samaras from a red maple develop and fall from the branches early. This picture was taken in May.

(*left*) Clusters of samaras from a white ash tree that have fallen to the ground in late September. The seeds are the narrow oval bulges closest to the twig.

SPIN SOME SAMARAS—OR MAKE YOUR OWN

If you do this activity outdoors in a breeze, the seeds can really move!

MATERIALS

- Maple samaras that have fallen to the ground (Red maple samaras fall as early as May and June.)
- Paper
- Drawing below right to trace
- Pencil
- Scissors

1. If the maple samaras you find on the ground are still paired, break them in half. (That way, they will spin better.)

2. Hold at least three or four maple samaras (the broken "singles") in your hand, high above your head.

3. Let the seeds go, and watch as they spin and whirl down!

Or: If you can't find any maple samaras (or it's the middle of winter), make your own following these steps.

1. Use the outline model below to trace or copy some samaras, and cut them out. The big samaras are from Norway maples. (Their actual size is nearly four inches across!)

2. Cut the joined pair in half, so you have two winged seeds. The much smaller samaras from a red maple are shown at the bottom, for comparison. (But they still spin!)

3. Hold the paper samaras above your head, and drop them. They will whirl and spin down just like real samaras! You can make as many samaras as you want—and drop a whole bunch of them!

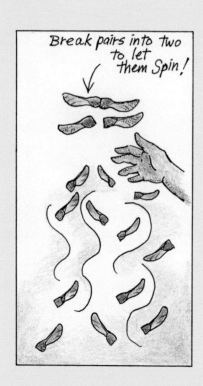

Break pairs into two to let them spin!

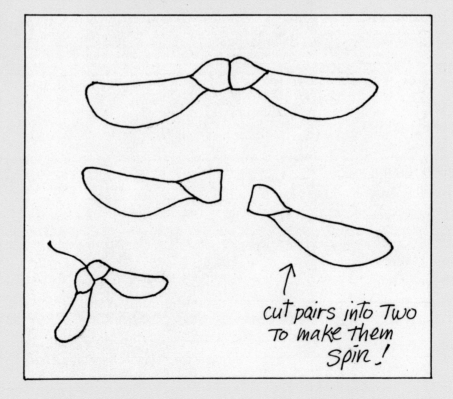

cut pairs into two to make them spin!

where a chipmunk or squirrel has sat and worked at finding the seeds. The cones of longleaf pine, eastern white pine, and pitch pine need two years to mature.

Not Just Nuts and Seeds

Many trees that are native to North America bear fruit in the form of small berries. The fruit usually has a soft outer pulp that birds and mammals can eat. The many species of hawthorn, mulberry, chokecherry, black cherry, dogwood, and serviceberry (also called Juneberry) have rounded fruits that ripen in the autumn and are eaten by wildlife through the winter. Cedar waxwings are among the birds frequently seen eating hawthorn berries. Purple finches

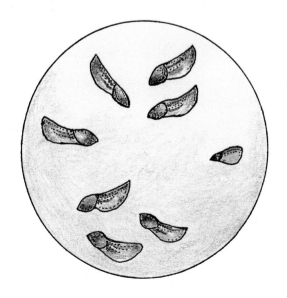

(*left*) The seven winged seeds from an eastern white pinecone (on the left) are just over one-half inch long. Compare the pine seeds with the one smaller seed on the right, from a red spruce.

(*top left*) The cones of a pitch pine are shorter and more rounded than the cones of a white pine. Each scale of the cone is tipped with a pointy spine.

(*top right*) The cones of an eastern white pine are about six to eight inches long.

(*bottom right*) Seeds from a black spruce (left). They are similar to the seeds of a pine, but smaller. On the right are seeds from an arborvitae, a conifer often used for landscaping near houses and offices.

feed on the dark fruit of serviceberries. And cardinals eat the berries of dogwoods.

Harvest Time

Once the trees have produced seeds, nuts, and berries, birds and other animals eat or collect the "harvest." By the middle or end of summer, cherry trees, hawthorns, and serviceberry trees have fruit on them. Later in September and October, the large nuts on hickory and walnut trees have already formed. The small cones of arborvitae and the larger cones of pine and spruce trees have also formed. From late summer and right through the winter, all this food from trees will be sought by birds, squirrels, deer, chipmunks, and other animals.

The fall is a beautiful time of year as the leaves of most deciduous trees, especially in the northern parts of the United States, turn yellow, orange, or bright red. Red maple is named for its scarlet autumn leaves. Quaking aspen and bigtooth aspen have leaves that turn yellow-gold. The leaves of black tupelo (pepperidge tree) turn deep red-purple. The star-shaped leaves of the sweet gum tree, which grows in the southeastern states, turn deep gold at first and then dark red-purple.

As fall approaches, the green color (**chlorophyll**) of leaves fades and disappears, and the substances (chemical pigments) that make other colors take its place—giving us an autumn treat of bright, colorful hillsides and woodlands. Trees in Canada and the northern United States are the most colorful. Many people plan their fall vacations in the hills of Vermont and other New England states so they can see the beautiful scenery.

Palm trees, some species of live oaks, and some acacias growing in the southern states or southern California remain green. Eucalyptus trees, native to Australia but planted in California, Florida, and Hawaii, remain green also.

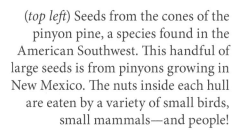

(*top left*) Seeds from the cones of the pinyon pine, a species found in the American Southwest. This handful of large seeds is from pinyons growing in New Mexico. The nuts inside each hull are eaten by a variety of small birds, small mammals—and people!

(*top right*) Purple finches feed on a variety of tree seeds and the fruit of serviceberry trees. This is a male.

(*right*) The fruit of a wild black cherry tree. This photo was taken at the end of August, when the berries were still ripening.

FOREST FOOD FOR ANIMALS

*Keep a lookout for food from the trees that animals could eat, and take notes. Notes and lists written "on the spot" outdoors are called **field notes** by biologists and naturalists. They are important records of what you have observed.*

MATERIALS

- Your sharp eyes
- Forest logbook and pencil
- Trees

1. Look at (and under) the trees in your neighborhood for seeds on the ground, nuts on the trees, or twigs with berries that animals might eat.

2. Look for birds, squirrels, or chipmunks near the trees, or on the ground under the trees, that seem to be looking for food.

3. Write down what you see in your forest logbook—even if you can't identify the tree. Write down the date and place, and whether the seeds or fruit have fallen to the ground or look fresh or dried.

Noticing Diversity

There are many different species of trees. You have already observed a wide **diversity** (variety) of shapes, colors, and textures of leaves and bark. In any forest or woodland, there is a diversity of tree species. A deciduous forest may seem to be mostly oaks, but maples and birches may be mixed in. The understory of a forest usually includes younger trees, but low-bush blueberry, sheep laurel, or hazelnut could be growing too. Small flowering plants on the woods floor may include several different species of wildflowers, ferns, and mosses.

A woodland also has a diversity of animals: birds, mammals, insects, spiders, reptiles, and amphibians—all with different shapes, sizes, textures, colors, and patterns. This wide range of diverse plants and animals is called biodiversity (bi-o-dih-VERS-ity). The biodiversity can be very different from habitat to habitat. The plants and animals living in a dry desert are different from those living in a swampy wetland. An ecologist studies the biodiversity of animals and plants that successfully live, feed, and raise their young in a habitat.

EVIDENCE OF FOREST MUNCHERS

As you take a walk in the woods, or even near street trees, you are likely to see evidence that birds or other animals have found food. You can write your observations in your forest logbook.

MATERIALS

- Your sharp eyes
- Forest logbook and pencil
- Area with trees

1. Look at the tops of stumps or rocks, or at the base of a tree, for a pinecone that a chipmunk or squirrel has taken apart. You might find a pile of scales from a cone, or a cone that has had half its scales ripped away.

This is where a chipmunk sat and took apart the cone of a white pine, scale by scale, to get at the seeds inside. All the scales are left in a pile.

2. Look for acorns on the ground. Some may have a small hole in the side from an insect. Others may have part of the shell chewed open and the nut inside eaten—probably the work of a mouse, chipmunk, or red squirrel.

3. Is there a hickory or walnut tree in the area? You may find that the nuts have fallen to the ground, with the greenish husks still on. Visit the area a few days later to see if the nuts are gone.

4. Do you see a lot of bird activity in a tree? In the fall, cedar waxwings visit hawthorns in small flocks to eat the berries. Cardinals come to dogwood trees to feed on the fruit. If you see a tree with lots of berries on it one day, revisit it a few days later to see if the fruit has been eaten.

Depending on weather conditions and

Two acorns have been chewed open by a red squirrel, leaving just the shells.

soil, trees produce more seeds, nuts, and fruit during some years and less during other years. It is important to write down what you find in your forest logbook, because you may not see as much the next year. Be sure to include the dates!

Are There Male and Female Trees?

Many holiday cards have a picture of holly berries, or winter holiday decorations using hollies. The red berries are produced only by the female holly. Female American holly trees and female English holly trees both need to have a male holly growing nearby. The flowers on the male trees produce tiny pollen grains, which have to reach the flowers on the female holly tree so the berry can develop.

Both American and English yew trees also bear male and female flowers on separate trees. English yews are frequently planted as landscaping shrubs or hedges and kept pruned and trimmed so they don't grow very tall. But just like the holly trees, pollen from the flowers on male yews has to reach the flowers on the female trees growing nearby. Box elder (a species of maple), ginkgo, and common juniper (a conifer) trees also have male flowers on one tree and female flowers on another. Sometimes people wonder why their holly or yew doesn't develop beautiful red berries. It's because their tree is female, and no male was planted along with it!

Pollen grains are very tiny—almost like dust—and can be spread by the wind; by insects such as bees, wasps, and butterflies; or even by hummingbirds. Most trees, shrubs, and small flowering plants depend on the wind or on pollinators to produce seeds, nuts, and berries. The flowers on many species of trees have both male and female parts in each blossom. Apple trees and hawthorn trees are good examples: each flower has tiny stalks called anthers, which have pollen grains on them, and a central stalk (the female part) called a pistil. Birches and many other species of trees have separate male and female flowers growing on the same tree.

7

Out and About— Tree Treks

Trees are almost everywhere you go: around your home, your school, and even parking lots. You'll be able to observe more trees if you can visit a city park, a bird sanctuary, or an **arboretum** (a special park for trees and other plants)—or go camping. A walk in a national park or a trip to a local lake or pond will give you the opportunity to see different types of trees in different habitats. Keep an eye out for the variety of birds, insects, mammals, and other wildlife you'll see along the way!

Visit a Park

A nearby city park is a good place to start to look at trees. You usually can find a map, leaflet, or website to learn about the trees in the park. Look at the information first, before you go out on a walk. It will help you be on the lookout for special trees, rocks, streams, or other landmarks. You don't want to miss anything!

Find out about the parks in your area. Ask your parent, teacher, or librarian to

PARKS AND FORESTS ON MAPS

Look at a local or regional map to discover where forests, parks, or sanctuaries are.

MATERIALS

- Map of your state
- Your sharp detective skills

1. Look on the map for areas outlined and colored in (usually in green), with a label of what kind of forest or park it is.

2. Look for other protected forest areas, such as a bird sanctuary, arboretum, or historic park or farm. Hint: Some parks and sanctuaries are called reserves.

3. Find other natural areas on the map, such as a river or pond, or landmarks such as rock formations. Look at how they are labeled or colored in, and it will become easier for you to find special places quickly on any map.

4. What is the nearest park or sanctuary to your home or school?

A trail curves into the woods. Many trails have handrails to lean on and benches to sit on.

help you find a map of your region showing where the parks are.

If you are able to visit a large state or national park, try to learn about it ahead of time. It will help to see a trail map first, so you can decide on the trails or areas that you want to explore. Most large parks have rangers or wardens who can answer your questions about special trees. Trails in large parks are often named for the trees that grow there: Tupelo Trail or White Oak Trail, for instance.

Don't forget parks that have historic buildings in them. Old buildings may have trees around them that are more than 100 years old. Guidebooks explaining the trees and other landmarks are usually available.

Around the Arboretum

You might have a state, national, or university arboretum (ar-bor-EE-tum) in your area. A local garden club might also have an arboretum. *Arboretum* comes from the Latin word *arbor*, meaning "a place where trees grow." Most arboretums have trails or walkways where you can stop and read signs about the trees there. Trees and shrubs—and even wildflowers—usually will have labels that identify each species.

(*left*) A walk along a woodland trail in the autumn can be a colorful experience. These are the brilliant leaves of a red maple.

(*center*) The leaves and acorns of a Gambel oak, seen along a trail in Utah.

(*right*) Trails at an arboretum give you a chance to see trees, shrubs, and wildflowers that you might not be able to see in your own neighborhood. This is a yellow lady's-slipper orchid.

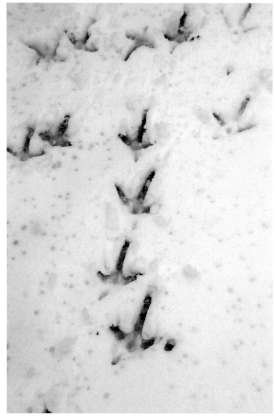

(*left*) Some parks organize special "full moon walks" so people can enjoy a guided moonlit walk in the park.

(*right*) Some nature centers and trail groups arrange special walks so the public can see evidence of wildlife in winter. These are the tracks of wild turkeys, in about two inches of snow.

Some arboretums have special "fragrance trails" with trees or shrubs that have different smells. Some also have rare or unusual trees. Be sure to get a trail map or guide to the arboretum so you don't miss anything! Arboretum staff can answer your questions or point out special trees and plants. Bring along your forest logbook and a pencil so you can take notes or make drawings, in case you don't get to visit that arboretum again.

Not Just for the Birds

Many communities have a bird sanctuary. Some are small, with short trails and easy walking paths. Others can be quite large, covering hundreds of acres. A bird sanctuary is a place where there are good habitats for birds to find food, rest and roost, and build nests safely. It might include open fields, woodlands near rivers or lakes, swamps, or deep forests. The sanctuary is a safe place where there are no roaming cats or dogs. Usually a trail manager or warden checks the trails every day. Some sanctuaries include gardens with flowers to attract hummingbirds.

But a sanctuary is not just for birds. It also might include habitats that protect other wildlife, such as frogs, toads, salamanders, rare butterflies, or mammals. As you walk around the sanctuary, you are likely to see a variety of animals, flowers, shrubs—and trees. Most sanctuaries have a trail map or a leaflet showing the different types of habitats it contains. The sanctuary staff members can answer questions, and they usually give "walk-and-talks" about the ecology and biodiversity of the sanctuary. So bring your forest logbook and a pencil and take field notes.

SOUNDS FROM THE TREETOPS

You learned in chapter 4 that a ruffed grouse needs to be alert to all the sounds in its environment. There are lots of sounds in the woodlands, if you listen up—higher up!

MATERIALS

- Natural area or sanctuary
- Your sharp eyes and ears
- Your forest logbook and pencil

1. When you are visiting a park or sanctuary, take time to simply stop and listen. (If you are talking, you won't be able to hear as much.)

2. Do you hear natural woodland sounds, such as birds or squirrels? Or can you hear an airplane, trucks, or a dog barking? Are other people talking?

3. Can you tell where most of the natural sounds are coming from? Warblers usually sing from the tops of trees. Vireos, tanagers, and orioles sing from high up also.

Baltimore orioles, like this male, are usually seen in the tops of trees.

4. On a hot summer day you might hear a cicada (sih-KAY-da). Cicadas are large winged insects that can fly up to the treetops. Male cicadas make a loud buzzing noise.

5. Write down what you hear in your forest logbook. You might not hear those same noises again soon. You don't have

to identify what the birds or insects are called, but your written field notes will help you remember exactly what you heard—where and when. In some years there are lots of cicadas, and in other years you might not hear many. The birds you heard in the spring may be gone later in the year.

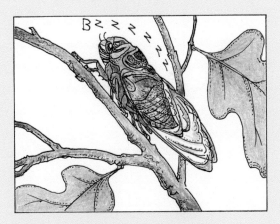

Several species of cicadas are found across North America.

Reading the Signs

Parks, sanctuaries, and campgrounds usually have signs telling you the names of the trails, where a special landmark is, or what direction you are walking. Signs also tell you about restrictions. You might come across a sign that reads NO CAMPFIRES, to prevent forest fires, especially during a drought. A NO PETS ALLOWED sign might be in the park because cats and dogs can be a danger to other wildlife. Some large parks may have signs asking you not to feed the animals. The restrictions are made to keep both the wildlife and the forest trees safe and healthy. Make sure you read all the signs when you visit a park or sanctuary, so you can be a true friend of the forest.

A flock of wild turkeys forage in a field at the edge of a forest.

On the Edge

In a large park or bird sanctuary, you might be able to observe **edge habitat**. A trail may take you along the edge of an open field or meadow, where it meets a forest. Deer, foxes, raccoons, and other mammals spend much of their time in the forest but also come out to the edge of the forest looking for food.

Birds also use edge habitat, especially for finding food. Flocks of turkeys often feed along the edge of a field, where there are plenty of insects to eat. They can still run or fly into the nearby woods and trees for safety.

Kestrels, which are small falcons found across most of North America, hunt for mice and grasshoppers in fields. But they need the nearby trees to find nesting sites. Kestrels nest in hollow trees, often using an old woodpecker nest at the edge of a field.

Other birds forage in the understory—smaller trees and dense shrubs that are at the edge of a forest. Blueberry shrubs, viburnums, and wildflowers such are partridgeberry growing on the edge produce fruits that attract birds. There may also be more insects. Many species of birds use the smaller trees and shrubs growing along the edge of a woodland as nesting sites. The

dense shrubs provide good cover for locating a nest.

Another type of edge habitat is found near lakes, ponds, or streams. At the edge of a pond you may see black willows, which have long, graceful branches. Shrubby species of willow and dogwood, along with alder and witch hazel, provide cover or feeding places for songbirds. Herons, ducks, kingfishers, and other birds find their food in water and make their nests nearby. Swallows fly back and forth over streams and ponds to snap up flying insects. Along the water's edge you may see beautiful dragonflies with glossy green or blue bodies.

Hovering over the water are mayflies and stoneflies.

At the edge of rivers and lakes, in both the United States and Canada, you might see river otters or beavers swimming in the water. You may also find the stumps of small trees that were chewed through and dragged away by beavers building their dams. Beavers chew down and collect large branches for their dens, or lodges.

The habitat along rivers, lakes, ponds, and streams is called **riparian** (ry-PAIR-ee-an) habitat. The ecology and biodiversity of riparian habitats is so interesting that some ecologists specialize in studying these areas.

(*left*) The edge of a pond is a great place to look for herons, ducks, and kingfishers.

(*right*) A "12-spot" dragonfly rests at the edge of a pond. The white patches on the wings are the 12 spots. This dragonfly is found across most of the United States and much of southern Canada.

FOOTPRINTS ON THE EDGE

In the soft mud or sand at the edge of a riparian area (a lake, pond, or river) you are likely to find the tracks of wildlife that come to drink or feed by the water.

MATERIALS

- Muddy or sandy area near water
- Your sharp eyes
- Your forest logbook and pencil

The footprints of a white-tailed deer, in soft, wet dirt. Notice the pointed front of each hoof.

1. Whenever you are in a riparian area (near a lake, pond, stream, or river), look for soft earth or mud where animals might have left their tracks.

2. Draw any tracks you find in your forest logbook. Try to estimate the size of a track and the distance between the tracks. You may not be able to identify the animal right away, but your drawings may help you, or someone else, identify them later.

Large birds like herons or crows leave tracks that have three forward toes and one back toe.

The front feet of many mammals leave a different imprint than the hind feet. Tracks from the front feet are usually smaller than those from the hind feet.

Camping Out?

If your family, school, or outdoor club is planning a camping trip, you might have a chance to observe new and different trees—and wildlife!

Most parks and campgrounds offer a map of the area. The campsites are often numbered, so you might be assigned to a particular site. Use the map provided to find out what direction north is. Don't be fooled by the old saying that "moss only grows on the north side of trees." Moss can grow on any side of a tree! And don't be misled by migrating flocks of birds heading north in the spring, or south in the

Trails are designed to let you walk easily through a forest and see the best views.

fall. They don't always fly directly north or south—they might be headed for a lake, shoreline, or another forest that is somewhat east or west.

Whether you are camping in a large park or a small one, remember to stay on the trail. Trails are designed to give the best views of trees, shrubs, wildflowers, and forest edges. Trails prevent people from squashing small plants that are rare or uncommon—and plants that provide food for birds and mammals.

You can make your own map of your campsite, whether it is in a large public campground or your backyard.

Go to School!

Many schools have trees around them. There might be trees planted around the parking lot or along the walkways and sidewalks leading to the school entrance. If they all look about the same size, they likely were planted at the same time. Many "street trees" planted near schools and office buildings and along city streets are cultivated varieties, or **cultivars** (KUL-tih-vars). They are trees that have been raised and grown for their shape, fall color, or ability to withstand drought. They have been grown from seed or from cuttings of branches from

DRAW A MAP OF YOUR CAMPSITE OR BACKYARD

A camping trip, even just overnight, will give you a chance to make your own woodland map.

MATERIALS

- Area to camp overnight
- Forest logbook or drawing paper
- Colored pencils, pens, or crayons
- Map of your campground or park

1. Start by making an outline drawing of the family car, if it is parked close by. Then add your tent and a nearby trail, trail sign, or road. (Hint: It's easiest to draw a bird's-eye view, as if you are looking straight down at your tent or the road.)

2. Add large natural landmarks, such as a nearby big tree or a large rock.

3. Look at the park map and find the compass sign that points north. Can you figure out where to add it to your own map? A park ranger or warden should be able to point to where north is, and to answer your questions about trees or special landmarks.

If you can't go camping, you might be able to camp in your own backyard and make a map of your campsite there!

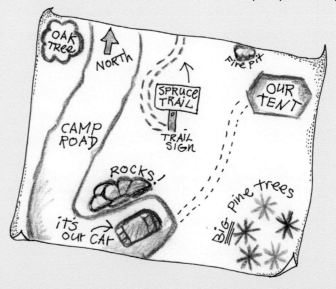

Rows of street trees are usually the same height, because they were planted at the same time. Red maples, white ash, and pin oak are common street trees.

Step Aside for "Leaves of Three"

A very good reason for staying on the trail at a park is to avoid brushing against poison ivy. If you touch this small plant, you can get a severe rash that itches, burns, and may even become infected.

Poison ivy is found across much of the United States and southern Canada. It grows along the ground on trailing stems, often creeping over old stumps and stone walls like a vine. It has three pointed leaflets and typically turns bright red in the autumn. In some areas of the central and western states, a similar plant called poison oak is common. While poison oak is not related to oak trees, its leaflets have a few slightly rounded lobes that remind some people of oak leaves.

The leaflets of poison ivy are often red-brown in the spring (when this photo was taken).

the healthiest trees. Cultivars are planted as shade trees and may be chosen because they grow quickly and have straight trunks.

Take a walk around your school (or apartment building or city park) and look at the street trees. Be sure to look at your local street trees to see if they all turn bright colors in the fall.

A Japanese maple, a native of Asia. It was developed as a cultivar for its color, which remains dark red throughout the year. It is frequently planted on streets, along parking lots, and near houses.

Are There Fossils of Trees?

There are many fossils of trees, but they are just the parts of trees. Fossils of tree leaves are common in some areas. In western Nevada, for example, lots of fossil leaves have been found that are about 16 to 20 million years old! There are fossils of oak leaves, along with fir, spruce, hawthorn, and hemlock. And there are even fossil seeds—maple samaras and pine seeds. In Wyoming, fossils of tree leaves and seeds (along with birds, insects, and even turtles) have been dug up. In Arizona, the Petrified Forest National Park has big chunks of fossilized tree trunks. Researchers have found fossil leaves of ginkgo (native to China) that are more than 100 million years old—and the leaves look the same as they do today!

Trees have been around for millions of years. If you could travel in a time machine and go millions of years back, you would be able to recognize the leaves of some of the same trees you see today near your school or in your own yard.

Amber is another type of fossil. Some species of trees produce resin, which is like a thick, sticky sap oozing from the bark. Millions of years ago insects that had been crawling on the trees or flying by got trapped in the sticky resin. The resin dried and hardened over millions of years, with the insect preserved inside, into a substance called amber. Since some amber is very clear, it's easy to see the insect inside. Fossilized amber millions of years old is found in many countries around the world including the United States, Canada, England, France, Poland, Japan, Russia, and the Dominican Republic.

A piece of amber (fossilized tree resin) from the Dominican Republic with a small ant stuck inside. It is about 25 million years old.

8

,,,,,,,,,,,,,,,,,,,,,,,,,,,,

People and Trees— and Forest Conservation

Around the world, people have given special names to important trees and forests. They also have discovered rare trees and rediscovered others that were forgotten. The forests in many areas are protected as parks and sanctuaries, but forested lands around the world need continued conservation efforts. Conservation groups help to protect forests by educating the public and by conducting research to decide which areas need to be preserved. When people learn about forests, ecology, and biodiversity, they are more likely to want to protect forests and wildlife. It's easy to learn about trees in your area—and to become a "tree keeper" yourself!

State Trees

Every state in the United States has an official state tree. Twelve provinces in Canada have an official tree. For example, the red oak is the state tree of New Jersey and also the provincial tree of Prince Edward Island in Canada. The paper birch (also called white birch) is the state tree of New Hampshire and the provincial tree of Saskatchewan, Canada. The southern magnolia (a species with large flowers) is the state tree of both Mississippi and Louisiana. The state tree of California is the coast redwood.

You may have already learned in school what your state tree is. Ask your teacher or librarian to help you find out what species it is.

Famous Trees and Forests Around the World

In many countries around the world, forests and even individual trees have become famous.

- A white oak in Connecticut was named the Charter Oak because in 1687, a group of early colonial leaders had to hide an important document—a charter—in the tree. They didn't want a British agent to find it!

- The General Sherman tree is the biggest living giant sequoia tree (by its estimated weight and volume).

- The tallest coast redwood (about 380 feet tall) is named Hyperion.

- You've probably read or heard about the legend of Robin Hood, who lived about 900 years ago in England. The forest he lived in (with his group of "merry men") was Sherwood Forest, which is now a protected forest park in England.

- The Black Forest of southern Germany is famous for stories of imaginary witches and werewolves. The forest got its name because parts of it are very dark and dense with conifers.

- In South America, the area around the Amazon River is famous for its rain forest.

(*left*) The leaves of a sugar maple, the state tree of New York, Vermont, and West Virginia, turn bright yellow-orange in the fall.

(*right*) The twigs of a young balsam fir, the official provincial tree of New Brunswick, Canada. Balsam firs are often grown on tree farms to be harvested as Christmas trees. The needles on younger firs lie somewhat flat, while the needles on older firs grow outward.

It's on a Street Sign Near You

Trees are important to a diversity of animals for finding food, making a nest or den, or resting and hiding safely. But trees are also important to people as symbols of strength, beauty, and long life. That's why we name many streets and towns after trees!

In California, there are towns named Cottonwood and Walnut

Creek. In Illinois, you can find the towns of Sycamore and Poplar Grove on a map. Florida has towns named Live Oak and Royal Palm Beach. And in Ontario, Canada, there is a town called Oakwood.

Most cities and towns have streets with the names of trees. Maple Street and Elm Street are common street names. Some towns have several streets named after trees. The city of Norwalk, Connecticut, has Tulip Tree Lane. You probably have a street in your own town or neighborhood named for a tree.

Many towns and cities have streets named after trees—like Elm Street.

On a road entering the Gros Morne National Park in Newfoundland, a World Heritage site.

- The Gros Morne National Park in Newfoundland, Canada, is a UNESCO World Heritage Site.
- The United States has several famous forests, including Adirondack Park in New York, Pinelands National Reserve in New Jersey, and Sequoia National Park in California.

These are only a few of the notable trees and forests around the world. There are many more! A kauri tree in the forests of New Zealand is at least 2,000 years old. A recently discovered spruce on Fulu Mountain in central Sweden may be the oldest tree in the world. There are more studies and more discoveries to be made every year!

It's ... Yew!

There are famous trees almost everywhere in the world. The Fothergall Yew—at least 2,000 years old—may be one of Scotland's oldest trees. There are several species of yew trees. They are usually called taxus (TAX-us) by landscapers and tree nurseries. The English yew is native to Europe and part of Africa. The Pacific yew grows in the extreme western United States and Canada, and a rare species grows in Florida. According to legend, Robin Hood of Sherwood Forest used a hunting bow made from yew.

DESIGN A POSTER ABOUT YOUR STATE TREE

You can make a colorful poster to help your friends and classmates learn about your state tree.

MATERIALS

- Photo or drawing of state tree
- Poster board, or a big piece of heavy white paper
- Colored pencils, pens, or crayons
- Old newspapers and magazines
- Scissors
- Glue
- Tape

1. Look at a photo or drawing of your state tree. Make your own drawing of the tree on your poster board. It should be the biggest part of the poster design.

2. Cut out words such as *Save!* or *Look!* from newspaper sales ads. Or cut out colored arrows or exclamation points. Glue them on the poster.

3. Write the name of the tree in big letters.

4. Tape or hang your poster in a place where others can see it. Ask your teacher if you can hang it in the classroom. When people see the poster, they are likely to ask you all about it—and you can tell them what you have learned!

Rare Trees

A species of tree may become rare because it has been cut down everywhere it grew, or because few are left due to widespread fires, drought, or even insect damage. The American chestnut tree became a rare species because a blight (a fungus infection) killed more than a billion trees. A tree may be rare in one state but not in another. The chestnut oak is a rare species of oak

in Maine, where it is at the very northern edge of its **range** (the place where it grows naturally). But it is found in several other states in the east.

In the southeastern United States, a small tree called Elliottia is very rare. It seems to spread mostly by its rootstock, which sends up new growth.

Lost in the Woods!

The Franklinia tree (named for Benjamin Franklin) is famous because it is extinct. There are no wild Franklinias left. Around 1765, John Bartram and his son William saw a stand of these beautiful flowering trees along a river in Georgia. The

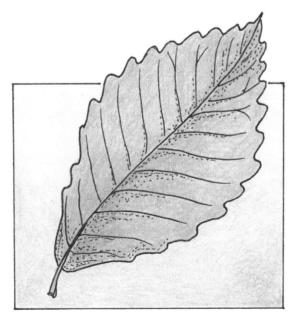

Bartrams were naturalists from Pennsylvania who were exploring the south. William Bartram explored by himself years later and collected specimens (seeds and roots) of Franklinia to bring back to Pennsylvania. The seeds and roots were cared for in the Bartrams' gardens so they would grow into saplings. The trees grew quite well, but the original stand of wild Franklinia was never found again. All of the Franklinia trees alive today (and sold in nurseries) are descendants of the original roots or seeds brought north to Pennsylvania.

In China, a species of wild magnolia has become extinct because all the trees were cut and harvested to make medicines. There are none left growing in the wild, but the trees are grown and cultivated in gardens.

(*left*) Scientists are developing cultivars of the American chestnut that will be able to resist the fungus that killed a large number of the trees. The tree's leaves turn yellow-gold in the fall.

(*right*) The leaf of a chestnut oak. This oak is rare in Maine.

Celebrate! Arbor Day and Earth Day

National Arbor Day is traditionally the last Friday in April. However, states that have long, cold winters observe Arbor Day (or even Arbor Week) on a later date, often in May, when it is warm enough to plant trees. Most towns and cities hold Arbor Day celebrations and events. Young trees (saplings) are often planted in front of a school or community building as a special event. The first Arbor Day was celebrated in 1872.

Earth Day, which began in 1970, is celebrated every year on April 22. Local events often include planting saplings and cleaning up litter. Some people even set up birdhouses. Both Arbor Day and Earth Day are welcome holidays for ecologists, conservationists, and environmentalists. The two days offer excellent opportunities to remind people of the amazing natural world around us.

Take some time on Earth Day or Arbor Day to look at the trees around you—even tiny seedlings. Seedlings are trees that have recently germinated (sprouted) from seeds. Seedlings a few years old may be only a foot or two tall, but they are the trees of the future! If you are walking along a forest trail or in a large park, you are likely to see seedlings. They might be just a few inches tall or about knee-high.

Forest Conservation

Forests and woodlands are important because trees (and all plants) produce oxygen. They provide food and nesting sites for birds, mammals, insects, and other wildlife. Their root systems protect soil from erosion and prevent flooding along rivers. People grow and harvest trees for food (such as apples, walnuts, and cherries) and use timber and lumber to build houses, furniture, and even pencils.

We need to protect and preserve forests using good conservation methods. Conservationists help to teach the public about saving and protecting forests and finding the best ways to do it. They work with state and government programs to decide which forests and woodlands should be set aside as parks or reserves. They help states or towns to protect forested areas for the future. A conservationist also finds out what animals and plants are rare or endangered in a forest. There is probably a conservation group in your state or region.

Most parks and large forested areas have fire towers. From the high tower, which usually is between 20 and 60 feet tall, a forest service worker or park warden has a bird's-eye view of the landscape. The warden can easily look for any signs of smoke or fire—especially during a drought or very dry weather.

This fire tower is 54 feet tall, and made of steel.

SEEDLINGS—THE FOREST OF THE FUTURE!

You can discover some trees of the future whenever you walk in a park or woodland.

MATERIALS

- Area with trees
- Your sharp eyes
- Forest logbook and pencil

1. Whenever you are walking on a woodland trail—or visiting a park, sanctuary, or arboretum—look on the ground for seedlings.

2. Write field notes about a seedling you find. Draw a picture of it if you can. Try to make a good judgment of how tall it is so if you can visit it a year later, you can see how much it has grown.

A seedling pine or other conifer is usually easy to spot. A seedling that's only a few years old will have a main stem—which will be a woody trunk some day!

Seedlings of deciduous trees (such as maples, oaks, and birches) may already have several branches when they are a foot or two tall.

This seedling of an eastern white pine is only seven inches tall.

Look for seedlings as you walk around a park or hike along a forest trail.

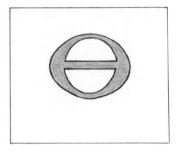

(*above*) This green oval design was the symbol for ecology in the 1970s. College students and environmentalists wore T-shirts or caps that had the green symbol on it. There were even flags with the ecology design!

(*center*) A landscaper fills in the last shovelfuls of dirt after transplanting a 10-foot-tall balsam fir on Arbor Day.

(*right*) A university student examines forest insects for his classes. He is using a stereomicroscope.

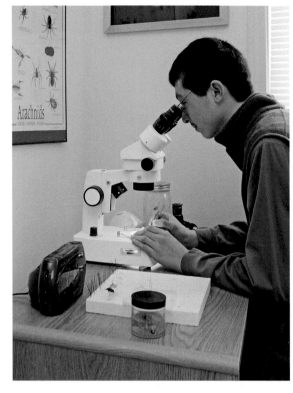

Tree Keepers

Many people work to protect our forests and city trees and keep them healthy. Here are some examples:

- Entomologists are scientists who study insects. It's important to know what species of insects can damage forest trees or street trees. Species new to an area may invade or infest a woodland as they arrive from other places. An entomologist knows how to identify insects (and trees) and determines if the range of harmful insects might be spreading to new areas. State and forest service entomologists often use light traps (traps that have special ultraviolet lights to attract insects) to collect and study forest insects.

- A botanist is a scientist who studies plants. A botanist can specialize in studying forest wildflowers, trees, the range of trees and shrubs, or how plants are affected by pollution.

- A **dendrologist** (den-DROL-uh-jist) is a botanist who studies trees and shrubs and usually teaches at a college or nature center.

- Ecologists study and evaluate how plants and animals live together in different habitats, such as swamps and deserts. Ecologists investigate the food and nesting sites that animals need and their relationship to the trees and other plants in that habitat. They also evaluate how the climate and soil affect the plants and animals.

- An arborist is a person who has had training in the best way to care for trees. Arborists know the best methods to prune and transplant trees and shrubs and how to identify insect damage or fungus infections.

- Professional landscapers know what types of trees and shrubs grow well along city streets and around homes, schools, and office buildings. They know the best way to care for the trees.

- Foresters work for state or national organizations to manage and analyze forest health conditions. They know how to identify insect problems and

A dendrologist uses a small magnifying glass to examine the new spring growth on a box elder maple.

What's That Leaf on the Canadian Flag?

The design of the national flag of Canada became official in February 1965. It has a bright orange-red maple leaf in the center. People usually call it a red maple leaf because it's red. But a leaf from a red maple tree has serrated edges. The leaf on the flag looks like a sugar maple leaf. Sugar maples are common across southeastern Canada and most of the northeastern United States. Sugar maples are also called rock maples or hard maples, because their wood is hard and heavy. The leaf on the Canadian flag is a stylized leaf, a design that was chosen as the best of many artistic designs. The colorful leaf is an excellent symbol of the bright and beautiful forested landscape of Canada, especially during the autumn.

Trees around the world are symbols of strength and long life, and are sometimes used as emblems on national or state flags.

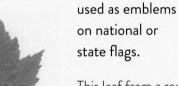

This leaf from a red maple has serrated edges.

winter snow and ice damage to trees, and they make decisions about new conservation efforts. Foresters often work with volunteers and conservationists to plant tree seedlings after a forest fire.

- Forest rangers, wardens, and foresters work at parks, forests, and state or other government agencies that protect and preserve trees. They often give educational tours and talks at parks.

- Wildlife photographers, nature artists, and outdoor writers help to teach the public about trees, forests, and wildlife by having their work published in newspapers, magazines, and books for all to see and enjoy.

- Most cities and towns have a tree commissioner or a tree warden who makes sure that the street trees are healthy and well cared for.

- Scientists and researchers who study climate, weather, and soils help us to learn more about keeping forests healthy. Recently, severe drought conditions have affected California and Nevada. Drought (a lack of rain) can last for years and can kill trees, shrubs, and grasslands.

 TRY THIS!

BECOME A TREE KEEPER

*Trees near houses, schools, and town buildings are usually cared for so they stay healthy. You can adopt a tree near your home and keep it watered or mulched. **Mulch** is a covering of dead leaves, pine needles, or grass cuttings (or a mix) spread around a tree to help keep the soil from drying out. If you look at trees planted near your school or an office building, you might notice a circle of mulch around the trunk.*

MATERIALS

- Tree near your home
- Watering can (optional)
- Rake
- Gardening gloves or work gloves

1. Ask an adult for permission to take care of a small tree or shrub near your home.

2. If it hasn't rained recently, you might need to water the tree first. Always check for any local water restrictions before you begin watering.

3. Mulch your tree. To make mulch, rake up a pile of leaves, cut grass, or pine needles (or a mix). Place them around the trunk. Use gloves to protect your hands. The mulch should be about 3 or 4 inches deep. Leave a space right at the trunk to keep insects away from the bark. For a young tree (a sapling), you can spread the mulch away from the trunk to where the branches above end.

4. Don't pack the mulch down—leave it loose. If it's very windy, you might have to water the mulch a little to keep it from blowing around. The layer of mulch will help keep the soil below from drying out.

Tree Terms

The forest has a thousand eyes
but you have only two—
And that is why the birds are wise
to everything you do!

Glossary

amber: Fossilized tree resin. Resin is similar to sap, oozing from a broken branch or from damaged bark. Insects and tree seeds can be caught in the sticky resin and completely preserved. Several sites around the world are known for amber. The amber from the Dominican Republic is about 20 million years old. Amber from Canada is about 65 million years old.

annual rings: Also called growth rings. As a tree grows, new layers of wood are formed each year. When a tree is cut down and the flat end of the stump is sanded smooth, you can see each year's growth as a ring or circle.

A veery rests on a balsam fir. The veery, found across most of southern Canada and the northern United States, is a forest bird with a unique song. The song is often described as a downward spiral, twirling rapidly downward like notes running down a spiral staircase.

arboretum: A public sanctuary for trees and shrubs. It's not a forest but a place where many trees and shrubs have been planted. Labels or signs identify each species. An arboretum may have rare trees or trees from other countries.

arborist: A tree-care professional who has had special training in planting, selecting, and pruning trees. Many large towns or communities have an arborist on staff, who can give the right care to trees that have been damaged in a storm or affected by insects.

botanist: A scientist who studies plants. A botanist might specialize in trees, shrubs, wildflowers, mosses, ferns, or other plants.

canopy: The upper parts of a mature tree: all the branches and twigs that support leaves. A sugar maple is a good shade tree because it has a spreading canopy that provides shade all summer.

carbon dioxide: A gas in the atmosphere that animals (including people) exhale. We breathe in oxygen from the air, and then we breathe out carbon dioxide.

catkin: A long dangling cluster of tiny flowers. Birch trees produce catkins with seeds, which are eaten by some forest birds. Many people are familiar with the shorter fuzzy catkins on pussy willow shrubs.

chlorophyll: The green coloring (a chemical pigment) in the cells of plants.

circumference: For trees, a measurement taken around the trunk, about four feet from the ground. Wrapping measuring tape around the trunk is the easiest way to measure the circumference.

conifer: A tree that produces its seeds in woody cones. Pines, spruces, and firs are conifers. While they often are called evergreen trees, this is misleading. Some conifers, like the tamarack (larch), have cones, but their needles are not evergreen—they turn yellow-gold and fall off in the autumn.

cultivar: A cultivated variety. A tree or shrub that is developed, propagated, and grown from a wild species for use in gardens or landscaping. Many different species have cultivars, including hawthorn, apple, and red maple trees.

deciduous: Trees that lose their leaves each autumn. Maple, oak, birch, and ash trees are examples.

dendrologist: A botanist who studies trees and shrubs.

diameter: The measurement across a circle. The diameter of a tree that has been cut down can be measured by holding a ruler or tape measure across the widest part of the stump.

diversity: The number or abundance of different species living in an area. The diversity of wildlife in a healthy forest is greater than the diversity in a small city park. The diversity of insects and birds in a swamp is likely to be much greater than in a dry desert.

drought: A lack of rain. A period of time when there has been no rain or very little rain.

ecology: A science that examines the animals and plants that live together in an environment. A healthy forest ecology includes trees, shrubs, wildflowers, ferns, and other plants that live there—and all the animals (such as birds, mammals, reptiles, amphibians, and insects) and other life that can find food and make nests or dens there. The ecology of an area also includes the climate and soil conditions.

ecologist: A scientist who studies ecology. An ecologist may specialize in forest ecology, desert ecology, lake and stream ecology, or the ecology of a special area like the Arctic.

edge habitat: The area where two different habitats meet, such as where a large field meets the edge of a forest.

entomologist: A scientist who studies insects.

environment: The habitat, climate, and soil conditions of an area.

fascicle: On a pine tree, the needles grow together in a bundle (the fascicle) attached to the twigs. Pitch pine needles grow in fascicles of three, but the needles of an eastern white pine grow in fascicles of five.

field notes: Written notes about what you observe outdoors. Good field notes include the date, time, and place of your observation—and even drawings made on the spot "in the field." Field notes and field drawings help to document what you have seen, because you can't remember everything!

heartwood: The inner wood of a tree. You can see heartwood on a tree that has been cut evenly across: there will be a darker central area, surrounded by the outer layer—the sapwood, which is lighter in color. Many species of trees do not show a difference in color, but red oaks usually do.

larva (plural: larvae): An immature insect. A caterpillar is the larva of a butterfly or moth. The larva of a beetle is usually called a grub.

mulch: A layer of old leaves, cut grass, or pine needles that is placed on the ground around a trunk. Mulch helps to keep the soil below from drying out, and is very helpful during a drought. You can buy "bark mulch" from a garden center.

native: Growing naturally wild. Blue spruce is native to some of the western states but is often planted in the east (as a cultivated variety) for landscaping. Weeping willows are native to China but are planted in many other countries because they are beautiful trees.

old-growth forests: Forests or stands where most of the trees are at least 100 years old. Some old-growth forests have trees hundreds of years old—or even 1,000 years old! Typically, no home construction, lumber cutting, or other damage caused by people is present in old-growth forests.

oxygen: A gas in the atmosphere that people and other animals need to breathe. Trees need some oxygen too, but they produce more oxygen than they need. Trees and forests are important in replacing oxygen in the atmosphere.

petiole: The leaf stem. The leaves of some species have a very short petiole, while the leaves of other species may have long petioles.

pollen: The tiny, nearly microscopic grains that are produced by the male parts of plants. On flowers, the pollen usually comes from the anthers, held on tiny stalks surrounding the central pistil (the female part).

range: The natural, normal area where a plant grows. The normal range of the black walnut tree, for example, does not reach into northern New England, but many have been successfully planted in the state of Maine.

riparian: Near or along rivers and streams.

samaras: Most tree seeds that have a wing or blade. Maple, ash, and spruce seeds are called samaras. Most pine seeds have wings but are usually not called samaras.

serrated: Saw-toothed. The leaves of red maple and American elm have serrated edges.

shrub: A plant that usually has several woody stems rising right from the ground. Shrubs typically grow less than 15 or 20 feet tall. (Trees grow taller and usually have just one main trunk.)

snag: A dead or decaying tree that has had its crown and branches broken off (sometimes by a lightning strike). The decaying trunk may remain upright for many years. Snags contain many insects, which are an important food source for woodpeckers and other birds. Woodpeckers will often peck holes in snags for nesting sites.

species: One type of plant or animal. The trees of one species have a similar leaf shape, bark texture, flower or seeds, and general structure. There are many species of maples, for example, and each one can be identified by the shape of its leaves, its overall structure and size, its type of bark, and the flowers or seeds it produces.

stand: A forested area or woodland of at least five acres; a kind of small forest.

strata: The different layers or levels of a forest where the plants and animals live. The bottom layer includes the dirt and leaf litter. The next layers consist of small plants like wildflowers; then the understory of woody shrubs; and then the highest strata, the upper canopy, which includes the branches and leaves at the tops of the trees.

tree: A tree usually has a single main trunk and grows more than 20 feet tall. (Most shrubs are smaller and often have several branch-like trunks.)

tuckamore: Groups of short, stunted balsam firs and spruces, found mostly in northern areas, and especially in Newfoundland, Canada. Blown by constant strong wind, even mature tuckamore firs are only about four feet tall.

understory: The plants and small woody shrubs that grow in the forest, under the taller canopy of the trees. Blueberry and azalea are good examples.

Common and Scientific Names

Trees are listed here by family, in the order you are likely to find in most field guides.

YEW FAMILY

English yew	*Taxus baccata*

PINE FAMILY

eastern white pine	*Pinus strobus*
pitch pine	*Pinus rigida*
pinyon pine	*Pinus edulis*
tamarack	*Larix laricina*
black spruce	*Picea mariana*
eastern hemlock	*Tsuga canadensis*
balsam fir	*Abies balsamea*

REDWOOD FAMILY

giant sequoia	*Sequoiadendron giganteum*
redwood	*Sequoia sempervirens*
metasequoia	*Metasequoia glyptostroboides*

CEDAR (CYPRESS) FAMILY

arborvitae (northern white-cedar)	*Thuja occidentalis*

PALM FAMILY

Florida royal palm	*Roystonia elata*

GINKGO FAMILY

ginkgo	*Ginkgo biloba*

WILLOW FAMILY

black willow	*Salix nigra*
quaking aspen	*Populus tremuloides*
bigtooth aspen	*Populus grandidentata*

WALNUT FAMILY

black walnut	*Juglans nigra*
shagbark hickory	*Carya ovata*

LAUREL FAMILY

sassafras	*Sassafras albidum*

BIRCH FAMILY

paper birch (white birch)	*Betula papyrifera*
gray birch	*Betula populifolia*
American chestnut	*Castanea dentata*

BEECH FAMILY

American beech	*Fagus grandifolia*
European beech	*Fagus sylvatica*

OAK FAMILY

white oak	*Quercus alba*
bur oak	*Quercus macrocarpa*
Gambel oak	*Quercus gambelii*
chestnut oak	*Quercus prinus*
red oak	*Quercus rubra*
pin oak	*Quercus palustris*

ELM FAMILY

American elm	*Ulmus americana*

MAGNOLIA FAMILY

southern magnolia	*Magnolia grandiflora*
tulip tree (yellow poplar)	*Liriodendron tulipifera*

ROSE FAMILY

common apple	*Malus domestica*
black cherry	*Prunus serotina*
downy hawthorn	*Crataegus mollis*

SUMAC FAMILY

poison sumac	*Toxicodendron vernix*

MAPLE FAMILY

red maple	*Acer rubrum*
silver maple	*Acer saccharinum*
sugar maple	*Acer saccharum*
box elder	*Acer negundo*
Japanese maple	*Acer palmatum*

LINDEN FAMILY

American basswood	*Tilia americana*

TEA FAMILY

Franklinia	*Franklinia alatamaha*

CACTUS FAMILY

saguaro cactus	*Cereus giganteus*

DOGWOOD FAMILY

flowering dogwood	*Cornus florida*

TUPELO FAMILY

black tupelo (pepperidge tree)	*Nyssa sylvatica*

HEATH FAMILY

rhododendron	*Rhododendron* (several species are cultivated for landscaping)
Elliottia	*Elliottia racemosa*

OLIVE FAMILY

white ash	*Fraxinus americana*

Resources

Many organizations, private groups, and government offices focus on forests, conservation, the environment, ecology, and wildlife. Here are just a few:

American Bird Conservancy
http://abcbirds.org

American Chestnut Foundation
www.acf.org

American Forest Foundation
www.forestfoundation.org

Arbor Day Foundation
www.arborday.org

Canadian Forest Service
www.nrcan.gc.ca/forests

National Audubon Society
www.audubon.org

National Emerald Ash Borer Information Network
www.emeraldashborer.info/

National Park Service
www.nps.gov/index.htm

Nature Conservancy
www.nature.org

Project Learning Tree
www.plt.org

Rainforest Foundation US
www.rainforestfoundation.org

Tree City USA
www.arborday.org/programs/Tree CityUSA/index.cfm

US Fish and Wildlife Service
www.fws.gov

USDA Forest Service
www.fs.fed.us

Teacher's Guide

Here are some "tree topics"—ideas for classroom activities, or independent assignments:

- Look around the classroom and list how many things are made from trees: desks, chairs, pencils, paper, and so on.

- What kind of wood is used to make Popsicle sticks? Hockey sticks? Guitars?

- How is maple sugar made?

- Look through recent newspapers to find articles about forests or about events that affect trees: a drought, a forest fire, clear-cutting in the rain forests, or insect problems. Discuss the effects or solutions.

- Some students may not have trees near their homes or apartments that they can observe closely, or safely. They could instead draw a picture of their "dream tree," an ideal "perfect tree," or even an imaginary tree from another planet!

- Ask students to create word scrambles of tree names, or a quiz with multiple-choice questions.

- Start a classroom "tree calendar." Students can write down the first dates that they see a tree in bud, flowering, or fully leafed out. In the autumn, they can add the dates when leaves begin to change color and when the first leaves begin to fall. During the next school year, new students can compare dates with the previous year's.

- Find photos of tall mountains and discuss why there are no trees above a certain altitude or latitude.

- Write a short poem about a tree or forest. It can be silly or serious.

- Discuss a problem in conservation: Is it important to preserve a forest or woodland, even if few people get to see it?

- Are there any trees in Antarctica? Why or why not?

- Find out what your state or local forestry service or environmental group is planning for Arbor Day or Earth Day.

- Learn about a park, reserve, arboretum, or sanctuary in your area: When was it first started?

- Find out about these naturalists and conservationists:

    John Bartram (botanist), 1699–1777

    Rachel Carson (environmentalist/biologist), 1907–1964

    John Fraser (naturalist), 1750–1811

    Aldo Leopold (conservationist/writer), 1887–1948

    François André Michaux (botanist), 1770–1855

    John Muir (naturalist/writer), 1838–1914

    Thomas Nuttall (naturalist), 1786–1859

    Henry David Thoreau (naturalist/writer), 1817–1862

- Discuss what these common phrases mean:

    Turn over a new leaf

    Let's get to the root of this

    Branching out

    He can't see the forest for the trees

    Strong as an oak

    Giant oaks from little acorns grow

    We're not out of the woods yet!

- Make a list of things that anyone can do to be a tree keeper (recycle papers and magazines, mulch or water trees, learn more about the weather and climate, learn about forest insects, let other people know about wildlife diversity in the forest).

- Recently, building "faerie houses" in the woods has become popular. Discuss why walking off the trails in the woods and collecting sticks may endanger ground-nesting birds. The activities may attract dogs and cats into the woods. Would this pose a danger to wildlife?

Bibliography

Denotes titles suitable for young readers. Most are field guides that are useful for all ages.

Books

Adams, Kramer. *The Redwoods: The Larger-Than-Life Story of the Noblest Plants on Earth*. New York: Popular Library, 1969.

Alden, Peter, et al. *National Audubon Field Guide to the Southwestern States*. New York: Alfred A. Knopf, 1999.

American Forest Foundation. *Project Learning Tree: Environmental Education Pre-K–8 Activity Guide*. Washington, DC: American Forest Foundation, 2003.

Angelo, Ray. *Concord Area Shrubs*. Cambridge, MA: Harvard University, 1978.

Arduini, Paolo, and Giorgio Teruzzi, eds. *Simon & Schuster's Guide to Fossils*. New York: Simon & Schuster, 1986.

Bent, Arthur Cleveland. *Life Histories of North American Gallinaceous Birds*. New York: Dover, 1963.

Berger, John J. *Forests Forever: Their Ecology, Restoration, and Protection*. Chicago: Center for American Places, 2008.

*Brockman, C. Frank. *A Guide to Field Identification: Trees of North America*. New York: Golden Books, 1986.

Carlson, Brian D., and J. M. Sweeney. *Threatened and Endangered Species in Forests of Maine: A Guide to Assist with Forestry Activities*. Orono, ME: Champion International Corporation, US Fish and Wildlife Service, Maine Department of Inland Fisheries and Wildlife, 1999.

Collingwood, G. H., and Warren D. Brush. *Knowing Your Trees*. Washington, DC: American Forestry Association, 1974.

*Coombes, Allen J. *Trees*. Eyewitness Handbooks. London: Dorling Kindersley, 1992.

Drummond, R. B., and Keith Coates Palgrave. *Common Trees of the Highveld*. Salisbury: Longman Rhodesia, 1973.

Emerson, George B. *Report of the Trees and Shrubs Growing Naturally in the Forests of Massachusetts*. Boston: Dutton and Wentworth State Printers, 1846.

Gerhold, Henry D., Norman L. Lacasse, and Willet N. Wandell. *Street Tree Factsheets*. University Park: Pennsylvania State University and USDA Forest Service Northeastern Area, 1993.

Gray, Asa. *Manual of Botany of the Northern United States*. New York: American Book Company, 1889.

*Greenaway, Theresa. *Tree Life*. Look Closer Series. New York: Dorling Kindersley, 1992.

Gullion, Gordon. *Grouse of the North Shore*. Oshkosh, WI: Willow Creek Press, 1984.

Hassinger, Jerry, et al. *Woodlands and Wildlife*. University Park: Pennsylvania State University Press, 1979.

Hunter, Malcolm L., Jr. *Wildlife, Forests, and Forestry: Principles of Managing Forests for Biological Diversity*. Englewood Cliffs, NJ: Prentice Hall, 1990.

Maine Forest Service, Department of Conservation. *Forest Trees of Maine*. Augusta, ME: 1995.

Maine Forest Service, Department of Conservation. *Forest Trees of Maine*. Augusta, ME: 2008.

Martin, Alexander C., Herbert S. Zim, and Arnold L. Nelson. *American Wildlife and Plants: A Guide to Wildlife Food Habits*. New York: Dover, 1961.

Mathews, F. Schuyler. *Field Book of American Trees and Shrubs*. New York: G. P. Putnam's Sons, 1915.

Northington, David K., and J. R Goodin. *The Botanical World*. St. Louis: Times Mirror, 1984.

Peattie, Donald Culross. *A Natural History of North American Trees*. Boston: Houghton Mifflin, 2007.

Perry, Philip. *The Concise Illustrated Book of Trees*. New York: Gallery Books, 1990.

*Peterson, Roger Tory, and Margaret McKenny. *A Field Guide to Wildflowers of Northeastern and North-Central North America*. Boston: Houghton Mifflin, 1968.

*Petrides, George A. *A Field Guide to Eastern Trees*. The Peterson Field Guide Series. Boston: Houghton Mifflin, 1998.

Pokorný, Jaromír. *A Color Guide to Trees, Leaves, Bark and Fruit*. London: Octopus Books, 1974.

*Ross, Andrew. *Amber: The Natural Time Capsule*. London: Natural History Museum, 2009. (It's somewhat technical, but the photos are fabulous!)

*Sibley, David Allen. *The Sibley Guide to Trees*. New York: Alfred A. Knopf, 2009.

Skelly, John M., et al. *Diagnosing Injury to Eastern Forest Trees*. University Park: Pennsylvania State University Press, 1987.

Spahr, Tim, and C. D. Kennie. *Incorporating Small Streams and Brooks into Developing Landscapes*. Wells, ME: Wells National Estuarine Research Reserve, 2005.

Standing Conference for Local History. *Hedges and Local History*. London: Bedford Square Press of the National Council of Social Services, 1979.

Stokoe, W. J. *The Observer's Book of Trees*. London: Frederick Warne, 1972.

Sutton, Ann, and Myron Sutton. *Exploring with the Bartrams*. Chicago: Rand McNally, 1963.

*Symonds, George W. D. *The Shrub Identification Book*. New York: William Morrow, 1963.

*Symonds, George W. D. *The Tree Identification Book*. New York: William Morrow, 1958.

Walden, Fred. *Dictionary of Trees: Florida and Sub-Tropical*. St. Petersburg, FL: Great Outdoors Association, 1957.

*Watts, May Theilgaard, and Tom Watts. *Winter Tree Finder*. Berkeley: Nature Study Guild, 1970.

*Zim, Herbert S., and Alexander C. Martin. *Trees: A Guide to Familiar American Trees*. New York: Golden Press, 1956.

Other Resources

Many booklets, magazine articles, newspaper articles, and monographs were studied to complete this book, as well as reports about trees and forests from radio or television programs. Examples include reports and newsletters from the Cornell Laboratory of Ornithology, the Arbor Day Foundation, the American Bird Conservancy, and the Nature Conservancy, and articles in *Northern Woodlands* magazine. In addition, maps and leaflets from several parks and refuges were studied.

The excellent seasonal reports from the Maine Forest Service (MFS) were vital, especially the *Forest and Shade Tree: Insects and Conditions* reports. Since 1993, staff members at the Augusta office of the MFS have been wonderfully generous in providing information about trees, forest pathology, insects, and weather problems.

For eight years, I operated an ultraviolet light trap to collect forest insects for the MFS surveys. This gave me the unique experience of observing the kinds of insects, and their numbers, that could be found on a mixed deciduous/coniferous woodlot. Finally, my own herbarium collection of botanical specimens, begun around 1985, has helped significantly in producing this book.

A young male white-tailed deer pauses for a moment to survey his territory in a Maine woodland. His antlers, still covered in "velvet," are only about six inches long.

Index

M

magnolias, 6, 16, 86, 89
maples, 4, 5, 9, 16, 26, 30, 32, *34*, 61, 64, 69
    box elder, *16*, 71, *93*
    Japanese, *83*
    Norway, 22, 65
    red, 6, *16*, 21, *32*, 34, 64–65, 66, 68, *75*, 82
    silver, *2*, *16*, 21
    sugar (rock), *4*, *16*, 21, 35, 46, 65, *86*, *93*
metasequoias (dawn redwoods), 12
mice, 39, *40*, 51, 55
mold, 55
moles, 39–40, *40*
mosses, 23, 30, 49, 52, *55*, 69, 80
moths, 41–42, *43*
    gypsy, 42
    luna, 41, *41*
    white underwing, *41*
mulberry trees, 64, 67
mulches, 94
mushrooms, 55
myrtles, 18

N

National Arbor Day, 90
needles, 5, 7, 12, 18, 27

nuthatches, 44–45, 50, 51, 54, 65
nuts, 61–64, 67–68, 90
    beechnuts (beech mast), 62
    black walnut, *62*
    shagbark hickory, *62*

O

oaks, 4, 5, 9, 16, 26, 32, *34*, 35, 41, 45, 61, 63–64, 69
    black, 7, *32*, 34, 63
    Charter Oak, 86
    chestnut, 89, *89*
    Gambel, *75*
    pin, 82
    red, 7, *57*, 63, 86
    Shumard, 46
    white, 5, *5*, *19*, 46, 59, 63
    Wye Oak, 59
olive trees, 18
orchards, 3, 61
orioles, 77, *77*
ovenbirds, 44
owls:
    great horned, 45
    screech, 50, *51*
oxygen, 7

P

palms, 14–15, 68
    Florida royal, *15*
parachutes, 64
parks, 74–75, 78
partridgeberries, 27, 38, *38*, 55, 78
pecan trees, 15, 62
pepperidges. *See* tupelos: black
petioles, 5, 19, 35
Petrified Forest National Park, 83
pine duffs, 26–28, *27*
pine siskins, 65
Pinelands National Reserve, 87
pines, 5, 12, 18, 26, 32, 35, *56*, 61, 68
    bristlecone, 59
    eastern white, *59*, *67*, 91
    lodgepole, 21
    longleaf (southern; yellow), 21
    pinyon, 68
    pitch, *13*, *18*, *67*
    ponderosa, 46
    red, 46
    white, 12, *13*, 21, *32*, 34, 46, 67
    See also conifers; evergreens
plum trees, 5, 16
poison ivy, 38, 82, *82*
poison oak, 82
pollen, 64, 71